Growing Up in the Ozarks

GROWING UP IN THE OZARKS

John E. Hult

Quiet Waters Publications
Bolivar, Missouri
2001

Copyright ©2001 by John E. Hult. All rights reserved. Printed in the United States of America. No part of this book may be used or reproduced in any manner whatsoever without written permission, except in the case of brief quotations embodied in critical articles and reviews.

For information contact:
Quiet Waters Publications
P.O. Box 34, Bolivar MO 65613-0034.
E-mail: QWP@usa.net.
For prices and order information visit:
http://www.quietwaterspub.com

ISBN 1-931475-04-0
Library of Congress Control Number: 2001117993

Dedicated

to the Memory of

My beloved parents,

RALPH AND GERTRUDE HULT

And

My "Big Brother,"

PAUL D. HULT

Contents

INTRODUCTION 9

VERONA (1928-1930) 11
   FROM EAST AFRICA TO SOUTHWEST MISSOURI 11
   FOURTH OF JULY 12
   MY FIRST SOLO SHOPPING TRIP 14
   GRANDPA AND GRANDMA COME TO OUR
      HOUSE 14
   FUN WITH COUSINS 16
   PAINFUL LESSONS 16
   ANOTHER REDHEAD JOINS THE FAMILY 18
   OUR BRAND NEW AUTOMOBILE 19
   "WHY ARE YOU LOOKING AT ME LIKE A
      WOLF?" 21
   THE FIRST DAY OF SCHOOL 22
   NANCY 23
   BUTCH JOHNSON 23
   A KISS OR A SPANKING? 24
   READIN', 'RITIN', AND 'RITHMETIC 25

BETHANY HOMESTEAD (1930-1943) 27
   THE BIG MOVE 27
   OUR FAMILY POPULATION EXPLOSION 31
   BLACKMAN SCHOOL 34
   THREE R'S, BLACKMAN STYLE 38
   MISBEHAVIOR AND ITS CONSEQUENCES 42
   FAMILY AILMENTS AND INJURIES 46
   "THE HEALTHIEST LARGE FAMILY IN GREENE
      COUNTY" 51
   NOSTALGIC MEMORIES OF OUR PARENTS 53
   A DAY OF TRAGEDY AND SORROW 61

CREATURES GREAT AND SMALL 63
"DEAR DIARY" (1935-1938) 69
ONE-HORSE FARMING 76
THE JOHNSON GRASS BLUES 81
NANNY AND HER KIDS 83
LIVING OFF THE LAND 85
APPLES! APPLES! APPLES! 89
THE OLD SWIMMING HOLE 96
"TAKE ME OUT TO THE BALL GAME!" 99
LEARNING BY DOING IN THE 4-H CLUB 103
MY SABBATICAL YEAR 107
GOLDEN WEDDING DAYS 115
BACK TO SCHOOL - 1938 124
THREE SPECIAL FRIENDS 126
"LEARNING TO DO, DOING TO LEARN" 130
FUTURE FARMERS OF AMERICA 132
FFA SUMMER CAMP, 1941 136
"YOU RUN FAST, JOHN, BUT TOO LONG IN THE
   SAME PLACE!" 138
MUSIC—MUSIC—MUSIC! 141
A HAPPY SUMMER IN MICHIGAN 144
HIGH SCHOOL GRADUATION 154
PEARL HARBOR—WORLD WAR II—FAREWELL
   TO THE OZARKS 158

INTRODUCTION

For many years I have considered writing about my childhood in the Ozarks. The following stories begin with our family's return from Africa and Daddy's call to the little church in Verona, Missouri, in 1928. These reminiscences cover the next 15 years ending with my being drafted into the US Army in 1943. They have been written especially for my brothers and sisters, our children and grandchildren. My siblings will remember some of these events differently than I have stated them. This is not a comprehensive family biography but a nostalgic portrayal of the experiences which were special and memorable to me. Reference sources include family letters, my sister Ingrid's book, On Our Way Rejoicing, occasional newspaper clippings, a diary which I kept from 1935-38, plus high school newspapers and yearbooks.

In many respects these were difficult years for our parents. I can clearly remember Daddy's frustration at not being able to return to West Africa. The combination of the drought and depression years made it terribly difficult to make mortgage payments and even to put enough food on the table for our large family. I can actually remember going to bed hungry during the height of the drought. Both Mother and Daddy were definitely underweight at that time and I believe it was because they didn't have enough to eat.

On the other hand I remember those years as a wonderful, happy time. There was no doubt that our parents deeply loved each other and each of us. They considered their human love as a gift from God and daily acknowledged and praised Him. We children cared deeply for and were proud of each other. The arrival of each younger brother and sister was a thrilling, happy experience. We loved school and enjoyed our friendly and generous neighbors. I wouldn't trade my family and my childhood with anybody else in the world. It was just great to have grown up in the beautiful Ozarks surrounded by such a special warm human environment.

VERONA (1928-1930)

FROM EAST AFRICA TO SOUTHWEST MISSOURI

Two years after returning from Africa my father received a temporary call to serve as pastor of a small Swedish Lutheran church in the Missouri Ozarks. He was still committed to his dream of returning as a missionary to West Africa. By then the national mission board of the church had decided to devote their efforts entirely to Tanganyika. Ralph Hult stubbornly tried to persuade them to open a second front on the other side of the continent where he had spent two years exploring areas of great need. Because the matter was still at an impasse, he agreed to accept the position in Verona. After growing up with Swedish immigrants in Nebraska perhaps Daddy considered going to the unfamiliar Ozarks as something of another foreign assignment.

When we settled in Missouri our family was made up of my parents and four children: Paul (6), Ingrid (2), Veda (less than a year) and me. We were a happy family with parents who daily expressed their love for each other and for their children by words as well as deeds. We had the usual sibling rivalries and scraps but I sincerely loved each of them. Big brother Paul let me know that he was the alpha male in our juvenile pack, but it was usually a fairly benign dictatorship. I was four years old and my memory potential was shifting into high gear. Until then, recollections were fragmentary, but many events of our first two years in the Ozarks come back to me now in great detail.

Verona was a small town which sprang up along the main railroad lines connecting St. Louis to Oklahoma City, Dallas and points southwest. It was situated on the northwest perimeter of the Ozark Plateau. The crystal-clear Spring River flowed north and west through town, originating from a large spring gushing out of a limestone cave a few miles south. The rolling hills surrounding Verona represented the eroded remains of the ancient Ozark Mountains. The attractive village centered around one main street with a handful of stores and office buildings. I remember that there were at least as many buggies and other horse-drawn vehicles as automobiles moving over the brick-paved surface. Several church steeples were visible from any point in town and a newly constructed one-story brick school stood on the highest hill. I don't know why the town had been named after a city in Italy. Perhaps it was christened by the Italian laborers who had constructed the railroad or worked in the lead mines not far west.

The Ozarks had been sparsely populated until after the Civil War. Most of the earliest settlers were descendants of Scottish, Irish and English immigrants to the southeastern states. They had gradually migrated westward as the eastern states became crowded. They were true Ozarkians with a unique 'hillbilly' twang to their speech. Their conversation was salted freely with such quaint old English words as 'nary,' 'reckon' and 'yonder.' With the coming of the railroads immigrants from Northern Europe were drawn to this region. The largest group in our county had come from Germany. Most of them had already developed neat and prosperous farms. A much smaller cluster of Swedish immigrants had settled near each other in and around Verona. They banded together to build the attractive little frame church to which my father had been called as pastor.

FOURTH OF JULY

Some of my most vivid early memories from Verona reflect the celebration of the Fourth of July. Daddy was intensely patriotic. He was proud of his Swedish heritage but first and foremost he was an American who dearly loved his country. He brought us all downtown to watch the parade along the main street. I can still hear the exciting music of the small brass band which led the parade. Daddy held me up to get a better view of the three ancient blue-clad veterans of the Union Army from the Civil War. Today they would probably be called the Grand Marshals of the parade. The crowd cheered and clapped as they passed by in a horse-drawn carriage.

The largest contingent was a squad of uniformed WWI veterans, by then middle-aged but still trim and snappy. A few of them wore their inverted wash basin helmets and all carried rifles on their shoulders. After the parade there were long and noisy speeches in the park. I thought we could have done without them but my parents listened attentively. We kids were mighty hungry by the time we got to our picnic with friends in the park on the banks of Spring River. I remember specifically going back for seconds of the scrumptious angel food cake.

For us boys the Fourth of July was synonymous with fireworks. In retrospect I'm a little surprised at Daddy's affinity for such a noisy celebration. This man, who had never owned a gun even in his seven years in the wilds of Africa, bought long-barreled single shot cap pistols for Paul and me. Each of us received a cylindrical cardboard container full of fat noisy percussion caps. We were delighted and filled the air with explosive noise and the pleasant odor of burnt powder. After a while I got tired of pulling the trigger and started putting caps on the sidewalk. Grasping my gun by the barrel I began exploding the caps by hammering them with the butt end. My new technique worked fine until I used too much force and broke off the barrel. I looked down in horror and broke out in tears. I ran with my mutilated weapon into Daddy's office where he was busy at his desk. Of course I expected that he could fix it for me. He tried to console me but indicated that the barrel couldn't be reattached. Then he showed me that the percussion mechanism still worked. I went back out and resumed firing but much of the fun of that celebration had melted away.

When darkness descended Daddy brought out a bag of firecrackers. Paul and I were too young for them so he lit them one at a time and for a few delightful minutes we were privileged to witness the little boy who had become Rev. Ralph Hult. For the final event of the evening he lit sparklers for us, one at a time, so we could enjoy them longer. Paul, Ingrid and I each tried to see which one could put on the most spectacular sparkler-waving performance. That ended the first Independence Day in my memory. None since has surpassed it in fun, excitement, and treasured memories.

MY FIRST SOLO SHOPPING TRIP

One day when I was about five, Mother was preparing lunch and found that she needed several things from the grocery store. I volunteered to go for her, knowing that the kindly owner had a big jar of peppermint sticks with which he favored small customers. Mother wrote out a list and placed it in an open market basket. She apparently wasn't concerned about my safety in our small friendly village with little traffic. No cash transaction was necessary because we had an account which was paid at the end of the month. I was proud that I was now big enough to assume such an important responsibility and hurried the five blocks to the store. The storekeeper smiled down at me as I reached in the basket to retrieve the list. To my horror it was missing, apparently having blown out while I was running. I had flunked my big opportunity and tears began to flow. The store had no phone so I had to return home in disgrace. Mother consoled me, wrote out another list and pinned it in my shirt pocket. This time all went well and I was rewarded with not one but three peppermint sticks which I proudly shared with Paul and Ingrid. Veda was too young to share in the loot.

GRANDPA AND GRANDMA COME TO OUR HOUSE

Another big event filed in my memory bank was the visit of Mother's parents, Grandpa and Grandma Jacobson. Traveling by auto from their home 400 miles away in Illinois had to have been a formidable adventure in 1929.

Up until then their longest motor safari had been 200 miles to St. Louis to see their son play major league baseball. They arrived late and drove past Sportsman's Park just as a baseball flew over the wall in front of their car. When they got into their seats they discovered that the ball which nearly hit their car had been a home run hit by their own son.

Mother was beside herself with excitement as they drove up our driveway. I can clearly remember the happy sound of Grandma's hearty laugh as she hugged each of us. I can even recall clearly the nice odor of the leather upholstery of their big old touring car.

Grandpa stood tall and straight in spite of his seventy some years. We grandchildren were intrigued by his mustache which tickled when he nuzzled us. He had been quite an athlete and taught his son Bill most of the skills which started him on a career as a star major league baseball player. By the second day of his visit to Verona he became restless and looked for something to do. Our lawn had been mowed but there was tall grass around the edge. Grandpa found an old-fashioned scythe in the garage and efficiently cleaned up the rough edges around our house. He warned us to stay clear but we were close enough to enjoy watching him smoothly and rhythmically decapitating the weeds. Grandma pitched in, too, helping Mother with the household chores as they carried on a lively conversation.

The most special treat of all came at our bedtime. Grandpa got out his fiddle and played us to sleep. His repertoire included lively versions of "Listen to the Mockingbird," "The Arkansas Traveler," and "The Irish Washerwoman." Grandpa had come from Sweden on a sailing vessel when he was seven years old. He remembered the sailors teasing him because he wore leather pants. When he was in his early teens he began working in the coal mines in Illinois. He continued until he had saved enough money to get married and finance a farm of his own. Somewhere along the line he bought a violin and taught himself to play. Before long he became much in demand to provide music for Saturday night dances. When my mother was in her teens she learned to accompany him on the piano. On another night at our house Grandpa took out his accordion and serenaded us at bedtime.

At that time I was nearing my fifth birthday and Paul had introduced me to the world of numbers. I had taught myself to write them from the page numerals in a book and was filling a notebook with them in consecutive order. Grandpa was sitting nearby reading the paper when I reached an obstacle. I looked up and asked him, "Grandpa, what comes after nine hundred and ninety nine?" He glanced at me with astonishment and burst out laughing. My first reaction was that he thought his grandkid was pretty dumb, but I was reassured when he told Grandma, "John has written his numbers up to one thousand and he hasn't even started to school!"

The end of their visit came all too soon. We were saddened as they loaded up and drove away. We didn't see them again until their Golden Wedding celebration in Illinois eight years later.

FUN WITH COUSINS

The only relatives we had in Missouri were Daddy's first cousin Viola Nelson, her husband Clarence, and children, Alice, Frank, Verner and Viola Ruth. They had moved to the Ozarks from Kansas several years earlier and owned a farm outside Verona on the Spring River. Daddy and Viola had grown up near each other in Nebraska and were good buddies. The Nelsons became a special part of our lives over the next two years and we especially appreciated our visits to the farm. Verner was my age and a fellow redhead so we enjoyed playing together. We particularly liked to walk down to the river to launch imaginary boats, try to skip rocks, catch tadpoles, build dams across a small spring, and splash in the mud. We also learned to catch crawdads by tying a rock and a piece of meat to a string and suspending it in the deeper water by the bridge.

Other major attractions at the Nelson farm were food and music. Aunt Viola was a great cook. She knew just what little boys liked to eat, such as angel food cake and pie. Uncle Clarence was a skilled musician, playing the piano and leading the music at our church. He also played lively tunes on the clarinet and saw to it that his children learned to play different instruments.

Clarence had several beehives near the barn and I remember the terrible day when one of their four horses knocked over a hive. The angry swarm stung and killed two of these beautiful animals which were so important in the farm work. The whole family was shocked and grieving. They obviously loved these animals and needed them badly.

PAINFUL LESSONS

I learned a few things the hard way in Verona. One day I was trying to keep up with Paul throwing rocks into the vacant lot across the street. With a mighty heave I hurled a stone the size of a golf ball with enough velocity to reach my target but with a serious misdirection. It sailed through our neighbor's front window with a sickening crash and a shower of broken glass. Moments later a huge man stepped out the front door and marched purposefully towards Paul and me. He walked right past us to our front door and knocked loudly. Moments later Daddy came out with this gentleman and walked over to survey the results of my crime. I received a serious reprimand but no further punishment. I suspect that my father felt that the penalty of my shock and remorse pretty much settled the account. He couldn't take it out of my allowance because we were living in an era preceding such enlightened benevolence for kids. I was grateful to Paul when he became my advocate, indicating that my target had not been the neighbor's window.

My big brother also introduced me to the demonic little-boy practice of catching flies, pulling off one wing and watching them struggle to fly. When Mother caught us she became quite upset and told us how terrible it was to torture any living creature.

Not long afterwards we were running barefoot in the yard. Honeybees were harvesting the nectar from the white clover blossoms. Mother warned us to stay away from them but they looked so much like harmless flies that I wasn't impressed. When she wasn't looking I deliberately stepped down on one who was diligently probing a blossom. Pow! The bee nailed me and I suffered sharp and awful pain. Of course I ran into Mother's arms. She was sympathetic but reminded me that she had warned me about bees. I decided that maybe I had better pay attention to what she said because she knew a few things that I didn't.

One night after we had gone to sleep we were awakened by loud voices. Somebody shouted to my parents, "The house next door is on fire!!" We rushed outside to witness spectacular flames shooting skyward and hear the angry roar and crackling explosions of an out-of-control blaze. The house was unoccupied at the time. Before the fire department arrived the building was almost consumed. The firemen quickly unreeled their hose and unleashed a stream of water which hissed noisily as it reached the flames. Fortunately the wind blew the flames away from our house so we weren't threatened. It was necessary to hose down the first house in the direction of the breeze and watch closely for secondary fires from the burning embers showering down for some distance. After the danger was past we were escorted back to bed but sleep didn't come soon. The following morning men came to comb the smoldering remains for evidence of arson. There had been a rash of similar fires at night. Some were thought to have been started to collect insurance by absentee owners desperate for cash in economically bad times. That night of experiencing the awful destructive power of fire is permanently etched in my memory.

ANOTHER REDHEAD JOINS THE FAMILY

Six days after my fifth birthday my sister Eunice was born. Paul and I had noticed changes in Mother's girth and she had informed us that we would soon have a new brother or sister. We were totally mystified about how the baby would arrive but weren't given any relevant information. I felt a special affinity for the new arrival because she came so soon after my birthday, and what little hair she had was bright red. Big blonde brother Paul may have been a little dismayed because he now had four younger carrot-topped siblings. From the start Eunice was a contented and happy little bundle. I was thrilled when mother let her be the first baby I ever held on my lap. Perhaps that was when I sensed an embryonic inclination toward becoming a pediatrician. I remember how pleased and proud my parents appeared to be. In the evening at bedtime we gathered around her crib and sang the lullaby hymn, "Hush, My Dear, Lie Still and Slumber." We all agreed that she was special and we still feel the same way.

Our family, July, 1929. Daddy, Paul, Mother, John; Ingrid, Veda, Baby Eunice at one month

Those were days of long confinements so Mother needed help. A young German girl named Hilda Osterloh from a nearby farm came to stay with us for a few days. We children immediately liked her friendly ways and she took good care of us. Her strange accent intrigued us but was no barrier to communication. Shortly after her stay with us she got married. I was just a little jealous of the young man who became her husband.

OUR BRAND NEW AUTOMOBILE

Our family was especially proud of our new Model-T Ford. I'll never forget how excited Daddy was when he drove it home for the first time and suggested that we take an outing. Mother prepared a picnic lunch. We all piled in with Mother and Baby Eunice in front and we four older kids in the back. We were all set for our maiden voyage. I was confused when Daddy walked to the front of the car but soon learned that the only way to start the engine was to crank it. After several unsuccessful whirls he came back and showed Mother how to adjust some levers on the steering wheel. This done he gave it another try and it kicked back at him. He got his arm out of the way quickly enough so there was no damage. In those days many men went around with right arms in slings or casts as the result of rebellious Fords. Finally we were treated to the staccato message that the engine was alive, and off we went.

As we rolled down the street I proudly waved at two of my friends. I believe we were the first family on our block to have a car. Our route took us out into the country and crossed a small creek over which there was no bridge. I was anxious when Daddy drove right into the water. How did he know how deep it was? I was relieved when we crawled slowly up the opposite bank. Later I was petrified when we reached Spring River and crossed over a wooden bridge with no side rails. It was barely wide enough for one car. I was certain that we were going to slip off into the water. But we made it safely and stopped on the other side for our picnic supper.

The return trip was much more relaxing and we returned home safely after a memorable outing. As I shut my eyes to go to sleep that night all I could see was that view out the car window of nothing but deep water as we crossed that narrow bridge.

The next spring, while Paul was still in school, Daddy asked me if I would like to go with him on a one-day trip to Branson. I was thrilled and eagerly accepted. Our destination was only about fifty miles away but it took us most of the morning to traverse the hilly route through the Ozarks. The beautiful green countryside was decorated colorfully at intervals with redbud and dogwood blossoms. Branson in those days was a tiny mountain village built around one main street.

Daddy's objective was a visit to the School of the Ozarks, a large residential facility with a farm and industrial arts complex. Poor families could send their children here to work their way through high school and learn a trade at the same time. Later it was upgraded into a college-level program and is now a respected institution of higher learning. The campus was situated on a bluff commanding a gorgeous vista of the White River three hundred feet below. The stream was later dammed a few miles downstream to form Lake Taneycomo. We enjoyed spectacular views as we were taken on a tour by one of the teachers.

The new Model T. Picture taken in 1933; Paul, John, Mother in the car; Carl, Veda, Ingrid, Baby Martha and Eunice.

The long walk exhausted me, and Daddy suggested that I wait in the car while he went into the office to visit. He was gone for what seemed like hours but was probably not more than fifteen minutes. Panic overwhelmed me and I was sure that something had happened to my Dad. I started crying loud enough for a kindly old man to come over to investigate. Others joined him and everybody tried to help. Somebody asked, "What is your father's name?" Between sobs I answered, "Ralph Daniel Hult!" My explicit answer elicited some friendly smiles. Just then Daddy returned, obviously alarmed at the crowd I had drawn, and remorseful at my distress. He thanked the people who were trying to look out for me and we headed home. I don't remember much of our return trip because I slept most of the way. I have special memories of that day because it was the only time I recall just the two of us doing something together in my preadolescent years.

"WHY ARE YOU LOOKING AT ME LIKE A WOLF?"

We were living in an era when major crime figures often made the headlines. Al Capone, John Dillinger, Pretty Boy Floyd and other outlaws were subjects of much discussion and concern. In 1929 our family had our own first-hand encounter with a notorious criminal. Our house was situated not far from the railroad tracks and almost every day, real-life hoboes would stop by and ask for food. Many were nice pleasant guys who were just plain hungry. Our parents never turned them away. Sometimes they would be asked to saw a few sticks of wood for our stove, but always they would be given a sandwich, a bowl of soup or leftovers from a previous meal.

One day a scruffy black-bearded man appeared at the back door with a large sack slung over his shoulder. In my mind's eye I can still see him, a ragged mean-looking dirty bum. But he was hungry and Mother was going to feed him! She went into the kitchen to fix something. In the few minutes of waiting we watched him suspiciously looking up and down the street. Suddenly he took off at a fast pace without waiting for his food. Perhaps he thought my mother was calling the police. This made Daddy angry. He ran after the man and grabbed him by the shoulder, scolding him for not accepting our hospitality. He wheeled on my father and shouted, "Why are you looking at me like a wolf?" Then he turned and hurried away even faster. Several neighbors stood by and watched this encounter.

A few hours later he was shot to death by railroad detectives who recognized him. His picture was published on the front page of our newspaper and he was identified as Jake Fleagle, a dangerous criminal. He was wanted for bank robbery and the murder of three people in Lamar, Colorado, a month earlier. If the neighbors hadn't been present he might well have shot our Dad.

Many years later I read an article in the Sunday supplement of the Denver Post describing the most notorious criminals in Colorado history. Jake Fleagle was one of those listed!

THE FIRST DAY OF SCHOOL

Starting school was one of the highlights of my days in Verona. We didn't have kindergarten so it was a matter of leaving the carefree life at home and plunging into the unknown new world of the first grade. I was so excited about that first big day that I didn't sleep much the night before and woke up earlier than usual. After our breakfast of oatmeal and toast, Mother helped me get ready. She adjusted my knicker pants at the knees, saw that my fly was buttoned, checked my ears for dirt and combed my hair. I proudly put on my sturdy new school shoes which emitted a nice little squeak if I stepped just right. Mother then handed me my lunch in a Karo syrup bucket and gave me a goodbye kiss.

Paul was by then an experienced third grader so he led me up the hill to the red brick schoolhouse. My parents had registered me earlier so my big brother only needed to show me to the door of my classroom. My heart was pounding with excitement and apprehension. We were a little late so most of the children were already inside. The teacher looked up and invited me in. I stepped forward but failed to notice that there was a six-inch step-down from the blackboard platform to the main part of the room. Not seeing this, I tumbled head over heels onto the floor and my tin lunch pail clattered and rolled right up to the teacher's desk. My spectacular entrance was greeted by a roar of laughter from my new classmates. I was embarrassed but at the same time enjoyed the attention. I grinned sheepishly, picked up my lunch bucket and proceeded to my designated seat.

The first period went by rapidly with introductions, seating assignments, and orientation by our no-nonsense but likable teacher, Miss Barker. The first recess found us busy trying out the playground equipment and conducting the important business of forming little cliques and establishing pecking orders. When the bell rang and we were re-entering the classroom I decided to see if my comic tumbling routine was good for another laugh. So I pretended to trip and roll on the floor as I had on my first entry. Again there was laughter but not as much. My thirst for acclaim and notoriety still wasn't quenched so I tried it again after lunch. By then Miss Barker had had enough. She declared in a loud voice, "John Hult! You've tried that trick once too many times already. There will be no more of that nonsense!" Believe me! It didn't happen again.

NANCY

My desk was in the back so I could observe my classmates without being too obvious. My gaze kept wandering back to a little girl, who had big blue eyes and bouncy blond curls. She was seated on the left side of the room about two rows ahead of me. I soon discovered that her name was Nancy and she had the most wonderful smile. She reminded me of a picture of a little angel we had on the wall at home. Every time I looked at her my heart went pitty-pat and I was completely smitten. Of course I was too shy to declare myself and I even avoided getting too close to her. Surreptitiously I watched her comings and goings and simply continued to worship her from afar. We moved to Springfield about a month later and I never so much as said hello to her but she lived on in my daydreams for a long time. I wonder what ever happened to Nancy, and where she is now.

BUTCH JOHNSON

There was a darker side to those first weeks of school and his name was Butch Johnson. He was a big tough-looking bully from one of the upper classes. The moment he laid eyes on me he strolled over, grabbed me by the front of my shirt and said, "You little redheaded shrimp! I'm going to beat you up!" He shook me like a rat but didn't deliver any blows. My friends were afraid of him so I didn't get any help from them. I was petrified but much relieved when he released me and said that he would wait until tomorrow to administer the beating. He sounded like he meant what he said. I avoided my dark destiny the next morning by waiting just outside the school grounds until the bell rang and then rushing directly into the building. We weren't allowed to stay inside at recess so I put Plan B into effect. I had discovered a gap in the foundation with a crawl space under the building. A little boy could easily conceal himself there. I slipped out and hid there until the bell rang for us to return to class. Of course this couldn't go on forever so I settled on the strategy of watching carefully for my tormentor and keeping out of his line of sight. He did catch up with me a couple more times but didn't do anything more than verbally abuse me. I was relieved when our parents told us that we would soon be moving to Springfield which meant that I would be fifty miles away from Butch Johnson.

A KISS OR A SPANKING?

Another predicament arose which was of my own creation. One day I was on the seesaw opposite a second-grader named Jimmy whom I liked a lot. He got into an argument with a classmate Susie who was seated right next to me. Insults were hurled back and forth and Jimmy finally said, "John! Kick her for me!" I was anxious to make points with him so I turned and gave her a sharp blow to the shin with my heavy school shoes. She ran screaming into the schoolhouse to our teacher. I knew that I was in big trouble and ran to my special hiding place under the building. There I trembled in awful trepidation even after the recess bell rang.

My absence was conspicuous so Miss Barker sent two of the bigger boys out to get me. They knew where I was hiding and I didn't put up much resistance as they dragged me back to the classroom. They led me in front of the 'judge' and court was in session. The grim-faced teacher asked, "John! Did you kick Susie?" There wasn't much point in denying it so I humbly admitted my guilt. Then the sentence was passed, "Either you remain after school for a spanking, or you can go over and kiss Susie and tell her that you are sorry!" I'll have to admit that I was a coward; I was flat out afraid of being the recipient of corporal punishment. And besides, I kissed my sisters all the time. What would be so awful about kissing another girl? Head down I walked over to her desk, gave her a quick peck on the cheek and said, "I'm really sorry, Susie!" I hadn't anticipated the reaction of my male classmates who tittered in glee.

After school was out I had to face the full force of their ridicule as the boys all sang out in chorus, "Johnny kissed a girl!--Johnny kissed a girl!"

And it didn't stop there. For the remainder of our time in Verona I was taunted every day from every direction. That was another reason I was happy to be getting out of town. Of course it meant that I'd never see my dream girl Nancy again but that pain would heal with time.

READIN', 'RITIN', AND 'RITHMETIC

The academic aspects of these first weeks in school weren't particularly challenging. Paul and our parents had already taught me to read, so the "SEE DICK RUN!" primer was a bit boring. Arithmetic at that level was easy and fun. My main frustration came from writing and drawing because of my primitive fine motor skills and poor coordination. I really envied my classmates who could already draw attractive pictures and color within the lines. We moved to Springfield before the first report card was issued. When it came in the mail I was terribly worried about what Miss Barker would say about me. My relief was profound when Mother told me that my teacher had written that I was a good student but a little on the mischievous side. That news wasn't anything my parents didn't already know.

BETHANY HOMESTEAD (1930-1943)

THE BIG MOVE

In the fall of 1930 we moved from Verona. My parents, who had fallen in love with the Ozarks, decided to establish a permanent home on a forty-acre orchard farm five miles southeast of Springfield, Missouri. Actually there were only thirty-eight acres because the Blackman rural school was built on the two-acre plot on the northwest corner, just one hundred yards away from our house. Early on, our new home was christened Bethany Homestead, after the biblical home of Jesus' friends, Mary, Martha, and Lazarus.

For small children, moving generates mixed emotions and memorable adventures. Sadness at leaving familiar surroundings and friends is subdued by a state of eager anticipation of what lies ahead. I remember vividly the fifty-mile trip with all seven of us packed in our Model-T Ford. Every available inch of space was crammed with personal belongings. We were accompanied by two trucks, one carrying all of our furniture and household goods. The other was loaded with a 12x15-foot chicken-house. Paul and I had been amazed to watch the movers winch it up onto the truck. With help, Daddy had recently built two of these poultry homes and wanted them for our new venture at Springfield. The truck would go back to get the second chicken house on the following day. We traveled in convoy and it seemed to take forever over the primitive narrow roads.

We finally arrived and drove slowly up the 100-yard driveway lined with red-hued hard maple trees on the left and golden-leafed poplar trees on the right. Then we got our first good look at our new house constructed of native field stone and roofed with green composition shingles. A sturdy oak tree just to the south of the house would provide welcome shade from the heat of the mid-day sun. Other oak trees were scattered around the large open yard which also contained four circular mounds about two feet high and thirty feet in diameter. Daddy had been informed that these were probably the lodge mounds of Indians who had lived there many years earlier.

But our house was so small, less than half as big as our parsonage in Verona! How would all seven of us fit into it? It had only three rooms, a small kitchen, a bedroom for our parents and Baby Eunice, and a larger dining-living room which would also have to serve as sleeping quarters for us four older children. Heating was provided by a potbellied wood stove and cooking was done on a small wood-burning kitchen range. Since there was no indoor plumbing, water had to be hand-pumped and carried from a deep well twenty yards from the kitchen door. A one-hole outhouse stood sentinel fifty yards south of the house.

We arrived fairly late in the afternoon and the first night was hectic. Trunks, boxes, and the old reed organ were stacked in the living room with just enough space left to put up a double bed and a table. Mother cooked a hot meal on a small kerosene stove. Soon after supper all four of us older children, ages two to eight, were put down for the night, sleeping crossways on the double bed. There was some debate as to whether we should lie alternately head to foot but Mother insisted that we all have our heads in one direction. We thought this was great fun and there was a lot of giggling and chattering before we said our evening prayers and finally settled down. We eagerly looked forward to investigating our new environment in the morning.

After breakfast the next morning Paul and I set out on a safari of exploration. The large barn with attached lean-to shed for livestock became our first destination and we climbed the ladder into the haymow. It still emanated the familiar and pleasant odors of horses and hay. We looked out the big door through which hay was hauled up into the barn and enjoyed the great panoramic view of the James River valley a mile to the southeast. Here too was a ready-made launching platform where two naughty brothers would later conduct their little duels to see who could pee the farthest.

Daddy had accumulated a huge library and decided that the hayloft was the only space large enough for its storage. The main part of the ground floor with large swinging doors was designated as our garage. A small gabled smokehouse which stood near the barn had been converted into sleeping quarters for the Negro servant who had served the previous owner. A long henhouse large enough to accommodate three hundred chickens was situated south of the barn. The pigpen had been located farther to the northeast, away from the prevailing winds, for esthetic reasons.

Most of Bethany Homestead was occupied by the orchard with over one thousand apple trees plus a few peach, plum, pear, and apricot trees. When we arrived a few ripe apples were still hanging on some branches and many more in varying stages of decay were lying on the ground. Paul and I went around sampling them and soon discovered those with the best flavor.

Our next objective was an external inspection of Blackman School. That morning Paul and I were the first pioneers of a new trail from our house through the orchard to the school grounds. Over the next fourteen years all ten of the Hult children would traverse that path many thousands of times. We liked what we found, a gabled white frame structure, larger than most rural schools, but still consisting of only one room. Nearby stood a coal storage building and a shed large enough to accommodate either the teacher's horse and buggy or her automobile. The boys' 3-hole wooden privy sat fifty yards east and the girls', the same distance southeast. Water was provided by a well with a hand pump near the front door. On the north and west borders of the school grounds stood rows of large maple trees suitable for climbing. Paul and I checked out the swing set and tried out the base paths of the softball diamond. We then returned home to report on our scouting expedition. I looked forward to our first day of school the following Monday with some anxiety, but I figured that I had learned some lessons from my mistakes those first weeks in Verona that I wouldn't repeat.

We still hadn't explored the portion of our new estate which had the most appeal to me, a fifteen-acre plot of virgin Ozark forest covering the southeast corner of our property. Around the edges stood many large graceful black walnut trees which we could see were shedding a generous harvest of their golf-ball-sized bounty. Oaks of several species predominated and were the largest trees in our forest. Many towered up to nearly one hundred feet with trunks over two feet thick. Dozens of hickory trees provided food for the squirrels who resided in nests we could see scattered through the woods. Sassafras groves had sprouted where larger trees had been harvested. We also found clusters of persimmon trees with their date-like fruit which became wonderfully sweet after the first frost. On the eastern edge of the woods we found traces of an abandoned wagon road which had been the main route of traffic down to the James River and settlements to the southeast in days long past.

On the western edge of the forest an earthen dam had been constructed which impounded a pond about fifty feet in diameter. Feeding it was a small spring flowing from under a limestone ledge. Paul and I would spend many happy hours in and around this murky little lake over the next few years.

This then was our new home. Today I marvel at how our parents managed to raise a family of ten children in that tiny little house during those difficult years. They couldn't have done it without their strong faith, perseverance, hard work, and a large measure of genuine love.

We children learned early on that each of us was important and had a niche to fill and a significant role to play. There never was a time when I didn't feel loved, cared for, and needed by my family. Inevitably we brothers and sisters had our share of squabbles, disagreements and rivalries, but these were always overshadowed by our deep feelings for each other. In the following pages I will record some of my memories of the excitement, the joys, and the trials of our years at Bethany Homestead. It was a great time to be growing up in the Ozarks!

The trees on the right were 'Birthday Trees' planted on the days of our births.

OUR FAMILY POPULATION EXPLOSION

When we moved to Springfield there were five little Hults. Eight years later there were ten of us, all spaced eighteen months to two years apart. Mother had always indicated that she wanted a large family. She became quite upset with her own mother's insistence each time a new little bundle of joy arrived, that enough was enough. I remember that we older siblings were always delighted with a new brother or sister. Both of our parents clearly communicated that a new baby in no way diluted their love for each of us.

Little brother Carl arrived on January 24, 1931, three months after we settled at Bethany Homestead. We knew that something was happening that night when 19-month-old Eunice was put to bed with us. That made five of us sleeping crossways on that double bed. Daddy picked up the receiver of the wall telephone with his left hand, cranked a handle with his right hand, and was soon talking excitedly. We couldn't hear what he was saying. About an hour later a giant of a man entered the front door carrying a large black bag. He gazed in open-mouthed astonishment at the squirming mass of five small children under one blanket. Daddy introduced him as Dr. Hogg, who was here to help us get another baby brother or sister. We older kids were taken aback and amused at the name 'Hogg' but were careful not to laugh when we heard it. The doctor advised us to be as quiet as possible and then went into the bedroom to see mother.

Things happened rapidly after that. We were horrified to hear our dear mother crying out in pain in the bedroom. Ingrid and I were just about in tears and big brother Paul did his best to comfort us. The ordeal seemed to last forever but after one particularly long series of cries and groans we heard a series of angry, lusty wails from an unfamiliar little voice. Dr. Hogg proclaimed loud enough for us to hear through the door, "It's a boy!" Then we could hear both Mother and Daddy laughing and crying in joy. A few minutes later, cleaned up and wrapped in a blanket, our new brother was brought out for us to inspect. Daddy informed us that his name was Carl Eugene. Dr. Hogg took out his little portable scale and pronounced his weight as just over eleven pounds.

We all agreed that Carl was just perfect. Though he was almost bald Daddy pointed out that the bit of hair he had was definitely blonde. This pleased Paul immensely because he would no longer be the only one without red hair.

Bessie Clark, a nurse friend in a nice white uniform came to stay with us for a week. We called her Aunt Bessie and thought she was special. She spoke in an authoritative but soothing voice with a wonderful Ozarkian accent. According to her strong Baptist tradition she called our parents 'Brother Hult' and 'Sister Hult.' Daddy always said that he would rather be called 'Brother' than 'Reverend.' These quaint titles for our parents amused us children but we had nothing but respect and affection for Aunt Bessie. She saw that Mother followed Dr. Hogg's orders to stay in bed for a week and gently but firmly kept us all in line.

I believe that Dr. Hogg's charge for the home delivery was twenty-five dollars. In payment Daddy delivered fresh Leghorn eggs to his house in Springfield for about two years. Carl's arrival aggravated the space situation in our little house. Our parents reluctantly decided that we older boys could sleep in the little converted smokehouse. Paul and I thought this was a great idea which would give us more space, freedom, and independence. It was cleaned, furnished with a wood stove, a double bed, two chairs and a small dresser. Our neat little fraternity house was soon christened "the boys' cottage." At first Daddy would come out to see that we were safely tucked in and comfortable. If we had problems we could easily run the few yards to the house. I don't remember ever having to go to our parents for help during the twelve years we slept in the boys' cottage. The only scary times occurred during violent thunderstorms with nearby lightning strikes.

Nineteen months after Carl's birth our sister Martha joined the family. She was followed at appropriate intervals by Gustav, Mary and David. Fortuitously they alternated girl-boy-girl-boy so we ended up with five brothers and five sisters. The five youngest were all blondes, all healthy, sturdy and bright. And each of them was loved and cherished equally. I don't remember details of the later arrivals intimately because we boys weren't sleeping in the house. All of the younger children weighed over eleven pounds at birth. Years later I was to remember those weights when we learned in medical school that women having large babies frequently developed diabetes later in life. And sure enough, at age fifty our mother developed that disease which required her to use insulin for the rest of her days. Amazingly she survived to the age of ninety-two.

These additions to our family necessitated more sleeping space. One of the small new poultry sheds had never been occupied by chickens. It was moved near the house, then diligently scrubbed and cleaned. This became a dormitory for the older sisters and was known as "the girls' cottage." Ingrid, Veda and Eunice decorated the inside attractively and were quite proud of their little sorority house.

During the depression there seemed to be some limitation in the size of families in our community. Our parents were certainly the most prolific in our school district. When Martha was born I was eight years old and totally naive about the facts of human reproduction. I proudly announced to a group of boys before school the next morning that we had a new baby sister. An eighth grader sarcastically commented that my parents must spend all their time in bed. He then suggested explicit details of their bedtime activity. I was incensed and retorted, "My mother and father wouldn't do anything like that!" Of course this elicited roars of raucous laughter and I was totally humiliated. I was vaguely aware of the fundamentals of animal propagation but somehow thought that humans were different. I was as naive as a Catholic nurse colleague who told me that the Sisters in parochial school had her convinced that pregnancy could be the result of being kissed by a man.

Five sisters and five brothers.

I am awed when I consider the simple logistics of raising this large family. Mother breast-fed all of us an average of nine months. When I gave a tribute to her on her eightieth birthday I indicated that this meant that she had produced at least 2500 quarts of milk. And furthermore, I continued, she had washed enough diapers to string a lineful of them clear across the Grand Canyon. Veda contradicted me here and indicated that the older sisters had washed a significant percentage of the diapers. My rebuttal to that was, "Yes, indeed you did, but after all it was Mother who started it all!"

BLACKMAN SCHOOL

My memory bank contains some exciting images of our first day at Blackman School. On that initial morning Daddy led Paul and me through the orchard and up the stairs into the schoolhouse. He introduced himself and us to the petite attractive young teacher, Miss Flo Young, and gave her our transfer credentials from Verona. She welcomed us with warmth and dignity. When it was time she had one of the older students ring the brass hand-bell and the student body filed in briskly and took their seats. Miss Young introduced us and indicated where she wanted us to sit. In Verona Paul and I had been in separate classrooms each with pupils of our own age group. In this new setting we were together with about thirty students from Grades One to Eight in one large room. At first I was awed by the presence of guys and gals who were twice my size. Some of them towered over our teacher but it was apparent from the start that she was totally in control. I hoped that none of the big guys had the bullying tendencies of Butch Johnson who had persecuted me in Verona.

Four rows of double desks filled most of the room facing the teacher in the front. The lower grades were situated on the left and big kids on the right. The space was well-lighted with big windows along the south and east walls. A large blackboard was mounted on the north wall along an elevated platform which also served as a stage. A Webster dictionary about six inches thick lay on a pedestal in a corner by the blackboard. Heat was provided by a furnace in the northwest corner. A water cooler in the front of the room was filled from the well with a hand pump outside and we all drank from a common tin cup. A small closet was provided for the teacher's personal items and there were wall hangers for our coats and caps. For music there was a piano and a hand-wound Victrola with a small collection of records. Our library occupied several shelves at the back of the room.

Teaching eight grades simultaneously was challenging but our new teacher had things well in hand. First and second grades recited together and we were known as the D Class. Accordingly each succeeding pair of grades worked together, with the seventh and eighth grades designated as A Class. Miss Young started with us little kids that morning. All the other groups were supposed to be studying while we performed. My first impression was that my previous class in Verona had progressed more rapidly those first few weeks so that reading and arithmetic seemed easier at Blackman School that first morning. There was a wide range of abilities in D Class. One girl named Cora was at least 13 years old. She had never learned to read and was retained in the first grade. She was a nice person and I felt sorry for her. She probably had a severe dyslexia, but Miss Young was following the rules of the day in holding her back until she could read. When she was sixteen she dropped out, got married and was soon raising a family.

Time went fast that first morning and it was soon time for recess. It so happened that I was the only red-head in school at that time and one of the older boys approached and derisively addressed me, "Hey, you little red-headed peckerwood!" That was the accepted terminology in the Ozarks, but I took exception and angrily replied, "It's not peckerwood! It's woodpecker!" That of course was a mistake and I was to hear that hated nickname thousands of times. I came to feel that I was a member of a persecuted minority. My friends soon came up with a more acceptable handle, 'Johnny Firetop.'

Sometime during that first week I had another humiliating experience. Shortly before recess I was smitten by a powerful urge to relieve my swollen bladder. I don't know if I was afraid of Miss Young or too embarrassed to call attention to myself. I thought I could hold out for a few minutes, but that was a major miscalculation! I held out as long as I could, and then nature released the floodgates. The seat of my new bib overalls was totally saturated. When recess arrived I had a serious predicament. I let everybody go out ahead of me so nobody would see that conspicuous dark patch of moistened denim. I edged my way out the back door.

Then I made the biggest mistake of all. I reasoned that if I turned somersaults all the way to the boys' outhouse fifty yards away nobody would notice the evidence of my incontinence. I proceeded to execute my plan. Of course it had just the opposite of the desired effect and everybody in the whole student body got several good views of my conspicuously soiled posterior. Loud roars of laughter followed me all the way to my destination. My state of total mortification prompted me to hide in the privy until the recess bell rang. I meekly sneaked back into my seat to another chorus of loud guffaws. Miss Young very sympathetically soothed some of the pain by saying, "John, you don't have to be afraid to let me know when you have to go."

Not all recesses and noon hours were as traumatic for me as that one associated with my untimely display of incontinence. We had a wide variety of recreational pursuits which varied with age, sex and time of year. Softball was popular with most of the boys and some of the girls. In the fall we played football without the benefit of pads. We did not have a basketball hoop but occasionally played volleyball. We had swings but I don't remember a sliding board.

At certain times of the year marbles was popular, especially a game in which 3-inch holes were dug in the ground in a pattern much like a croquet court. The object was to shoot your marble into each one of the holes. Another marbles game was called 'Keeps.' Each player put a given number of marbles in a circle about three feet in diameter. Then we took turns trying to knock marbles out of the circle and got to keep the ones we knocked out. This game was outlawed because my classmate Warren McCallister had soon won all the marbles and some of his victims weren't happy losers. One day I visited Warren at his house and he gave me a demonstration of his phenomenal prowess with his 22-caliber rifle. He repeatedly tossed a tin can in the air and invariably put a bullet through it before it hit the ground. He was also the champion 'Rassler' of our peer group.

Another activity we really enjoyed was simply rolling auto tires. In those days they were much lighter and easier to handle than present-day models. We had to be careful though because they were still heavy enough to knock down a small child. We also had fun propelling metal hoops with sticks.

A somewhat dangerous game was called 'Mumbletypeg' in which a jack-knife is tossed in various ways to make it stick in the ground.

One of my friends unintentionally stabbed himself in the foot and had to get patched up. The name of the game derived from the original rule that the loser had to pull a peg out of the ground with his teeth. We didn't bother with that formality.

A popular group game was called 'Andy-over.' Half of the group stood on each side of the schoolhouse. One participant threw a rubber ball over the roof. If a member of the opposite team caught it he or she could run around the building and try to hit an opponent. The one hit had to join the opposite team. This continued until everyone was on one side.

One year we had a gentle giant of an eighth grader named Neil. He towered above everybody including the teacher. I think he was at least 16 and quite intelligent. He hadn't been able to finish grade school because his help was needed on the farm. We called him 'doorbuster' because he was so strong he had pulled a stuck outhouse door right off its hinges. He was kind and gentle with everybody, especially us little guys. We liked him to take the lead when we played 'Follow the Leader' because he was very creative and athletic. He would run backwards, crab-walk and even walk on his hands while we tried to repeat his antics in a long line behind him. One day we were running along, following him when he jumped up and kicked a wooden post supporting the volleyball net. It snapped right off near the base, nearly hitting me. He became something of a legend in our little fraternity. We really hated to see him drop out of school when he was needed again on the farm.

Most of us male students made our own slingshots and had all sorts of variations for target practice. One of the worst crimes we committed with them was breaking the glass insulators on telephone poles. Of course we learned early on that none of the teachers at Blackman School would tolerate the use of such weapons on the premises.

We had a row of large maple trees around the school yard which were wonderful for climbing. I had a real fear of heights when climbing ladders or nearing the edge of a cliff. Yet somehow climbing trees didn't bother me. As long as I could grasp a branch or hug a trunk I was fine. Several of us boys competed to see who could climb the highest. I was even crazy enough to hang by my legs when well off the ground. I had a wonderful recurring dream in which I would climb high into a tree in front of my friends and then launch into flight. Somebody would yell, "Look! John's flying again!" I would fly around the school yard waving at them until the teacher would come out and command, "John Hult! You come down from there!" That was one of my most delightful dreams and I had it with slight variations on several occasions.

The girls had their own set of group games such as London Bridge to which the boys were not invited. Both us boys and the girls were quite resourceful in entertaining ourselves and usually dreaded the ringing of the bell to bring us back inside.

THREE R'S, BLACKMAN STYLE

For the most part we Hult children loved school. Our parents had instilled in us the desire to learn and were eager to have us share our learning experiences with them. Both Mother and Daddy were adept at answering questions and amplifying the facts we had picked up in class. They also used the stimulus of having us reason out answers to questions in a logical manner and encouraged us to use reference books. Another reason I appreciated school attendance arose from the fact that it provided respite from all the chores at home. This was particularly true in late summer when there was so much to do on our farm and orchard. We just couldn't wait for school to begin again.

Coping with twenty-five to thirty students in eight different grades in one room presented an enormous challenge to one teacher. I liked and appreciated all three of the teachers I had during my years at Blackman. Each had her own style but had to follow a prescribed curriculum which emphasized the basic three R's.

I also remember geography, history, and simple biology subjects. Right from the start we little kids couldn't help but overhear the recitations of the upper classes and passively absorbed some of their material. I thought their lessons were much more exciting than our little Dick and Jane stories.

One day when I was in the second grade I got carried away stretching my neck to see what one of the third grade boys in the row to my right was reading aloud for the class. He was stumbling on some of the words and I was pronouncing them silently to myself. Miss Young noticed me and had the faltering reader hand the book to me. Then she suggested that I read the paragraph aloud for everybody. I proceeded to do so with no hesitation on the big words. Today I'm ashamed of my conceited showing-up of my bigger schoolmate, but there were no recriminations then. He was a nice friendly guy and didn't take offense. The teacher's next step was to pronounce, "John, you are now in the third grade. Move over into the C-Class row."

Skipping a student into the next grade was a fairly common practice at Blackman School. If the teacher was convinced that the pupil knew the basics and perhaps was not being stimulated enough she had the option of promoting him or her on the spot. This format was popular with many of the parents at that time. They had no intention of sending their children on to high school, so skipping a grade meant that a boy could get out to help his dad farm a year earlier. Accordingly a girl could get back to domestic duties and perhaps be ready for marriage sooner. I was pleased and proud but I believe my parents had mixed feelings about my unscheduled promotion. Sixty years later when I visited Flo (Young) Creighton she told me that she had given up the practice of skipping students soon after she advanced me. She had concluded that the extra year of school was important in many ways, especially for boys.

Handwriting drills were emphasized in the lower grades. First we learned to print. Then we had to fill whole pages of cursive script as nearly matching the beautiful letters mounted above the blackboard as possible. My fine-motor coordination was poor and I couldn't match the efforts of most of my schoolmates. My handwriting remained bad enough in later years to get me into medical school. The same lack of skill handicapped my efforts in art classes. My attempts at freehand drawing were terrible and I envied friends who could effortlessly create attractive pictures.

I thoroughly enjoyed reading and spelling. According to my diary I only misspelled two words on the daily assigned drills during the whole school year of my fourth grade. Aside from our textbooks the school library contained about one hundred books, mostly well-worn. By the time I graduated I had read them all, some of them several times. Funding provided for only four or five new books each year. When they arrived we fought over who was going to check them out first.

Each of our teachers tried to convey to us a certain amount of music appreciation. Flo Young used a set of Victrola records to teach us a variety of songs. Patriotic songs were a must including "America," the national anthem, etc. Many of the Blackman families were of Scottish and Irish lineage so we learned such numbers as "Loch Lomond," "Comin' Through The Rye," "We'll Mae The Keel Row," "I'll Take You Home Again Kathleen," and others. My favorite snappy number was, "Frog went a'courtin'. He did ride. Rinctum by mich-a cambo." There was another which made a deep impression and which I still carry with me today. Sometimes when I'm alone and down in the dumps I sing it aloud to myself. The first verse goes like this:

    Sing a little song when you are happy.
      The birds all do!
    When their hearts are glad they tell it.
      Why shouldn't you?
    Ripples on the water widen.
      Sunlight comes from far away.
    Sing a little song when you are happy.
      Be glad today!

I have never seen this song in any book, but can still hear a sweet soprano voice singing it to us from that scratchy old Victrola record.

One special memory of our big brother Paul stands out. When he was in the 6th grade the teacher persuaded him to sing a solo at our Christmas program. I think she must have twisted his arm a little. I'll never forget seeing him stand up on the stage in his new bib overalls with an angelic expression on his face singing,

    "I heard the bells on Christmas day,
    Their old familiar carols play.
    And wild and sweet the words repeat,
    Of peace on earth, Good will to men."

Paul went on to sing all the verses by memory in a clear soprano voice which was absolutely beautiful. We were so proud of him. We never heard him sing another solo. He didn't think he was good enough and was never one to blow his own horn. That just wasn't Paul's style!

The lower grades at Blackman School had what was called a rhythm band made up of a motley assortment of noisemakers including tambourines, triangles, kazoos and bird whistles. Each student was assigned an instrument and vigorously performed in time with a special record on the phonograph. The sound we produced was just awful, but I suppose it did stimulate our sense of rhythm and working together.

Sue Conrad Highfill was an accomplished musician and had us perform an operetta each year she taught. When I was a sixth grader she wanted me to play the male lead in the musical "Aunt Drusilla's Garden." I loved singing with others but was too self-conscious to perform alone. Furthermore, the role called for a couple of duets while holding hands with the female lead. I just couldn't see myself on the stage singing alone with some girl's hand in mine. So when we had the auditions I deliberately sang off-key and the starring role was given to my friend Donald Ingram. When Nina Esther Lattiner, the prettiest girl in school, was assigned the lady lead part I admit having had some second thoughts. Over fifty years later when I looked up Mrs. Highfill in retirement she said, "I'm still mad at you, John! You could have had that part, but you just wouldn't try!"

During my last two years at Blackman School I entered an obnoxious state of unblushing adolescent vanity. I had read all the books in the library and been exposed to all the curriculum materials more than once. Literally I was of the opinion that I knew more than anyone in the building including the teacher. We had just studied what little was then known about the magnitude of the universe and I was sharing this knowledge with Mother. She added a few details and then asked the question, "When you look up at the sun, the moon and the stars and know the vastness of our universe how does it make you feel?" My immediate reply was, "It makes me feel that I know a lot." Mother chided me gently and declared, "It makes me aware of how tiny and insignificant we are in the greatness of God's creation." As I progressed onward through high school, college and medical school I discovered how limited my knowledge was compared to the other students, teachers, professors, and scientists around me. And the greatest of them were usually the quickest to assert that the more we learn the more we find out we don't know. Today I realize how much I owe those three conscientious teachers at Blackman School for their patient contributions to those formative years of my life. I also learned a lot about life from my schoolmates and still cherish the memory of their friendship. Those were special years in my life!

Student Body 1932-33, grades 1-8, Flo Young, teacher. John, row 1, 2nd from right. Paul, row 2, on right. Ingrid, row 2, 3rd from right.

MISBEHAVIOR AND ITS CONSEQUENCES

All three of the teachers I had at Blackman School maintained a high level of discipline. If you misbehaved you were punished, and the severity of the offense determined the nature of the punishment. If you didn't complete your lessons you might have to stay after school to accomplish it. Other infractions might call for writing out on the blackboard one hundred times such penitent statements as, "I will never again carve my initials on my desk." Another punishment called for standing in the corner with your nose in a circle drawn on the blackboard. An alternative penalty involved standing in front of your peers holding the huge Webster's dictionary until your arms were painfully fatigued.

When I was about eight years old I was given a snappy-looking gray golf cap which I proudly wore to school. At recess I discovered that by holding the bill and flipping it horizontally it sailed like a present-day Frisbee. As I practiced this technique I noted that it flew farther if there was a more vertical trajectory. One careless aim propelled the cap up onto the roof over the front porch of the schoolhouse. I couldn't get it down myself and didn't have the good sense to ask for help. When we went home for lunch Mother asked me what I had done with my new cap. I then made the terrible mistake of lying that one of the big boys, Wilbur Davis, had thrown it up on the roof at school. In the afternoon this bald-faced fabrication somehow got back to our teacher. She scolded Wilbur and he angrily accosted me. In abject misery I admitted my guilt which turned Miss Young's wrath in my direction. She decided that this was an infraction which needed to be dealt with by my parents and gave me a note to take home after school. Wilbur easily climbed one of the porch supports and retrieved my cap. He accepted my apology, but let me know that he would beat the tar out of me for a repeat offense.

I still had to face the music when I returned home after school. Mother read the note and handed it to Daddy. He assumed responsibility for the next step and took me into the bedroom. I expected a spanking but almost with tears in his eyes he told me how disappointed he was that I had betrayed his and Mother's faith in me. He took down from his bookshelf the big black Lutheran Hymnal and turned to the liturgy which is repeated every Sunday in the worship service. He handed it to me and asked me to read aloud to him the section on the confession of sins. Part of it reads, "We are by nature sinful and unclean, and have sinned against Thee by thought, word and deed," Daddy then reminded me how terrible it is to tell lies which hurt others. He insisted that on the following morning I repeat my apologies to Wilbur and Miss Young. Finally he assured me that I was forgiven, but bore a great responsibility not to repeat such an offense. That episode made a more indelible impression on me than any amount of physical punishment would have. It remains one of my fondest memories of Daddy's caring love.

Corporal punishment was definitely a part of the code of discipline at Blackman School. All three of the teachers we had there over the years practiced it regularly. They probably would have been considered remiss in their duties if they hadn't paddled a few of us. I did not escape this painful indignity either but had only one encounter. In the second grade my seatmate, Warren McCallister, and I had things to share which just couldn't wait until recess. Several times we whispered to each other and Miss Young became aware of it. She warned us that if she caught us again she was going to spank us. After a few minutes of good behavior we lapsed and she spotted us in the act. We were called to her desk where, one at a time, she laid us across her lap and administered a dozen sharp noisy blows with the palm of her hand to our denim-protected posteriors. Warren was no stranger to this kind of medicine, having taken many previous doses. He didn't let out a peep but I reacted differently. The humiliation and physical pain triggered a deluge of tears. I also received further verbal punishment when the news filtered back to my parents.

Another form of physical chastisement the teachers used consisted in a few whacks with the ruler on the palm of the culprit's hand. I only remember this alternative being used on me a couple of times. My impression was that it was effective, a stinging blow to both the hand and the ego. Spanking with the teacher's bare hand followed relatively minor infractions, or you might say misdemeanors. More serious felony-grade offenses called for a real 'whoppin'' with an appropriate implement. At Blackman School the perpetrator was expected to provide his own instrument of punishment. The teacher pronounced the sentence with an ominous command such as, "Leslie! Go cut yourself a switch!" (Believe it or not, all of us boys carried pocketknives in those days.) The culprit would then march out to the edge of the schoolyard and pick out the sapling of his choice. And it had better be big enough or he would have to make a return trip! None of the rest of the student body enjoyed the public spectacle of a schoolmate being whipped. I vividly remember the awful sound of a limber switch impacting tender human flesh. Most of the miscreants appeared humiliated, but there was a wide spectrum of reactions to the pain, from stoic acceptance to subdued anger to copious tears. Girls weren't supposed to be immune to this level of punishment but I don't remember it ever happening. We boys thought this was definitely an example of gender discrimination.

I escaped this higher degree of chastisement but on one occasion had a good scare. As we were filing out of school for recess one day I was teasing one of the girls meanly enough to get her really upset. I was calling her by a nickname which she hated. Mrs. Strong reprimanded me rather sharply, but that seemed to be the end of it. A few minutes later on the playground two of my friends, Sidney Ingram and Howard Black, cornered me with a grim announcement. They had heard the teacher scolding me and decided to pull a fast one. They knew that I was easily taken in. With a straight face Sid said, "Mrs. Strong told us to tell you to cut a switch and bring it to her after recess." I was still feeling guilty and that my punishment really hadn't been completed. I went to a peach tree with some long saplings growing up from its roots. With my pocket knife I cut one which was at least four feet in length with a quarter inch base and a long limber tip. When the bell rang I let everybody precede me into the building. Then I sheepishly appeared at the door with my sleek weapon. The classroom became totally quiet and Mrs. Strong turned to see why everybody was staring. Her mouth opened in astonishment and she asked, "Why John! What's that for?" I explained that I had been instructed to bring it to her. She burst out laughing as did the entire student body, especially my two so-called friends. I might possibly have forgiven them if it had been April Fool's Day. The teacher didn't even bother to ferret out the source of my misinformation. Perhaps she reasoned that my gullibility needed to meet the real world.

One day my friend Jimmy Miller was caught making funny faces at the girls. He was warned, but repeated the offense when he thought the teacher wasn't looking. She caught him again and sentenced him to stand on her desk and make faces for the benefit of all of us. He was embarrassed but started enjoying himself when we couldn't help laughing. Suddenly the room became quiet; Jimmy's mother had walked in the front door behind him on an unscheduled visit. He couldn't understand why we were quiet and made his funniest facial contortion. By then his shocked parent had walked far enough forward for Jimmy to see her. He burst into tears of total humiliation. Mrs. Miller approved of the teacher's punishment, and he told me later that aside from a scolding there was no further discipline at home. She apparently decided that enough was enough.

I was in about the fifth grade when Mrs. Strong became our teacher. She was a stimulating pedagogue and I was applying myself rather diligently to my studies with no black marks on my deportment for the first few weeks. Then one day a friend hit me right in the face with a paperwad propelled by a rubber band. It smarted and I retaliated. Unfortunately my projectile ricocheted off my buddy's head and hit Mrs. Strong on the arm. With an ominous inflection she commanded, "Would whoever shot that paper wad please come to the front of the room!" I knew that there were many witnesses and that it would be futile not to comply. With head hung low I walked slowly forward. She appeared surprised and said, "Why, John Hult! You of all people! I can't believe that you would do such a thing!" My punishment was to stay at my desk for fifteen minutes after school which I considered a rather lenient sentence. When Mother asked my sisters why I was late they informed her of my infraction. This led to a high-level tongue-lashing when I did get home.

FAMILY AILMENTS AND INJURIES

As we grew up on Bethany Homestead we had our share of aches, pains, bumps, bruises and encounters with the nasty bugs which afflict small children. Visits to a doctor's office were almost nonexistent, only for desperate situations. Our parents were well qualified to deal with most of the ailments we children suffered. In preparation for Africa Daddy had taken a six-month course in basic tropical medicine for laymen, and Mother had spent a year studying and observing health care at Immanuel Hospital in Omaha. Then they had been on their own, far away from regular medical services for seven years in Africa. They certainly didn't pretend to be health professionals but had enough knowledge and experience to deal with most of our day-to-day medical problems. I firmly believe that they possessed the wisdom and common sense to know when they should call for help.

My most dramatic and scary memories of ill health grew out of our family epidemic of whooping cough in 1931. Several of our classmates at Blackman School came to class with terrible coughing

GROWING UP IN THE OZARKS / 47

attacks. Either Paul or I soon brought the bug home. Over the next three months, all six of the Hult kids were filling the house with paroxysms of unstoppable staccato barking. This was followed by a desperate gasping and noisy intake of air known as the whoop. Many times this brought on gagging and vomiting. Mother rubbed our chests with Mentholatum or Vick's Vaporub and dosed us with several different kinds of unpleasant tasting cough medicine. Our parents were clearly alarmed.

In 1925 they had seen many African children die from whooping cough. When it reached the Machame village near our Tanganyika home, Mother, Paul and I were moved to Shigatini, another mission station a few miles away. We stayed there until the epidemic had run its course.

Six years later in Missouri our folks tried in vain to keep newborn Baby Carl isolated from the rest of us. He became by far the sickest member of our household. In those pre-antibiotic times doctors had little to offer in the treatment of whooping cough. I can still hear Carl's awful unending coughing paroxysms followed by vomiting and desperate noisy intake of air. His plump little body rapidly wasted away to little more than a skeleton. Mother would let him rest briefly after an attack and then nurse him again. This was repeated over and over and over again. I distinctly remember Daddy leading us in praying earnestly for our dear little brother. After many trying days those prayers were answered as Carl slowly recovered. He grew up to be over six feet in height and over two hundred muscular pounds. He became a good middle distance runner and even played some college football. Years later Mother told me that at no other time had she been as afraid of losing one of her children than when Carl had whooping cough.

We kids loved to go barefoot in the spring and summer in spite of the rocky Ozark soil and a variety of thorns lying in wait for our feet. There were blackberry thorns, hawthorns, wild rose thorns, locust thorns and several others. In a letter to Grandma Matilda on May 31, 1935, I wrote, "Everybody here is all right. The only irritations I know are that we boys have a few thorns in our feet." When we stepped on them our parents were quite adept at picking them out with a flamed needle and fine tweezers. If they got infected Mother would have us soak the foot in hot water with Epsom Salts. Then she would apply Gray's Ointment, a dark paste smelling of linseed oil, to the puncture site. This was supposed to draw out the thorn and it usually worked. I also had a series of large painful boils, and Gray's Ointment was Mother's standard remedy to bring them to a head.

Mother had something of a fixation on the importance of daily intestinal elimination. In our house that bodily function was termed 'baya' which was the Swahili word for bad. Up until school age if one of her children hadn't performed for twenty-four hours she would get out the enema syringe and take corrective measures. Of course we all hated that. If this didn't achieve the desired results, she would supplement her therapy with a dose of castor oil. In my opinion that was even worse than an enema. The purpose of castor oil was "to clean out all those poisons." For this reason she also used castor oil with diarrhea, "to chase out all those nasty bugs."

In my teen years I had ridden my bicycle to the Ozark Empire Free Fair about ten miles from home. While there, I was suddenly smitten by a severe attack of nausea, cramps and diarrhea. After several trips to the bathroom I realized that it was time to hurry home to milk the cows. I was desperate and figured that I needed some kind of medication and only knew of Mother's favorite cure-all. I stopped at a drug store, bought a small bottle of castor oil, held my nose, took a big swig, hopped on my bike and hurried homeward. What followed became one of the longest, most painful and distressing trips of my life. There was no public restroom in that ten mile stretch but fortunately there were several stretches of thick woods along the road. That was the last dose of castor oil I took until about fifty years later when my doctor insisted it was necessary to prepare me for a certain x-ray procedure. I vowed that if I ever became a father I would find an alternative to castor oil for my own children.

On only one occasion during all those years at Springfield was I taken to see a doctor. At about nine years of age I sustained a small puncture wound on my right thumb. It was nearly healed when the whole thumb started swelling. Day by day it grew worse with terrible throbbing pain. Hot soaks didn't help and I could see that my parents were getting worried. One day I insisted on going to school in spite of the misery. We had a little rhythm band in which I played a tambourine. When I shook it the pain became almost unbearable but somehow I managed to finish the practice. That night I slept fitfully awakening every time I moved my hand. The following morning Daddy took me to the doctor's office in Springfield. I don't remember his name but this friendly middle-aged man took one look at my swollen digit and said that something had to be done. He took me into a little treatment room which smelled strongly of some kind of antiseptic. I was seated in Daddy's lap with my hand resting on the treatment table. The physician painted my thumb with iodine and then reached into a tray to pick out a sharp gleaming scalpel. Without warning he plunged the blade deep into the most swollen part of my thumb. The excruciating pain brought an agonized scream with copious tears, and pus spurted out of the wound. With the pressure relieved, the underlying throbbing ache soon subsided and I was tremendously grateful to my doctor. He wrapped my thumb and told us how to take care of it. I believe his charge was five dollars which pretty much emptied Daddy's billfold. The thumb healed completely but I still have a scar as a memento of that painful time. I didn't encounter another doctor face to face until my army induction physical exam about a decade later.

Our parents were rarely ill. Occasionally Daddy's back would give him trouble, a condition he called lumbago. We could tell that he was in pain but he kept on going without ever complaining.

Mother never seemed to be ill and only managed to have some respite from her hectic schedule when she was confined to bed for a week after delivering a baby. There was one terrible exception!

In June 1942 Daddy was on the high seas sailing for Africa. At the time we didn't know it but he was on a ship carrying munitions. He had been on the ill-fated Zam Zam in 1941 when it was sunk by a German raider. America was not yet at war with Germany so Daddy and all US citizens were released. Then a few months later our dauntless father got passage and was again attempting to return to his beloved Africa. We were anxiously awaiting news of his safe arrival in Capetown when Mother got sick. She had pulled a tick from her armpit a few days earlier and began to notice swelling, pain and fever. These symptoms progressed and she really began feeling miserable. She called Dr. Knabb in Springfield and he telephoned a prescription to the drugstore for the new miracle drug sulfanilamide. Mother asked me to drive in and pick her medicine up. I met a couple of high school friends at the drugstore and wasted time visiting with them so that it was nearly three hours before I got home. I didn't realize how ill and in what terrible distress Mother was. I was shocked to find her in tears. Not only was she desperately ill but also worried that I had had car trouble. She had always said that mothers couldn't afford to be sick and I guess I took her at her word. Never had I felt more ashamed of myself. I had failed her in her moment of great need.

In spite of the medication Mother was definitely worse by the following morning. Her temperature was higher and the angry swelling in her armpit had become huge. Even more scary for us children was the fact that she was becoming delirious. I drove into town to get 16-year-old Ingrid who in many respects was more mature and resourceful than I. She was living with and helping a couple from church who were imminently expecting a baby. Paul was in Illinois working in a defense industry-based job so Ingrid and I were the oldest children at home. We called Dr. Knabb who made a house call and insisted on hospitalizing Mother immediately. He called for an ambulance which also doubled as a hearse. All nine of us siblings were in tears as we watched two men load our wonderful mother onto a stretcher and drive away with her. Little David was only four at the time. How could this be? Mother had always been a tower of strength in our family.

Mother became critically ill and was in the hospital for four weeks. Dr. Knabb established the diagnosis of typhoid-like tularemia otherwise known as rabbit fever. Sulfa drugs are not effective against tularemia bacteria and Mother may even have had a reaction to sulfanilamide which made her worse. One night in her feverish state Mother had a vision that Daddy had been at her bedside the night before. She said that he had disembarked from his ship in Recife, Brazil, and caught a mail plane to Springfield to be at her bedside. He could only be with her for a short time before he had to catch his plane back to his ship in Brazil and resume his voyage to Africa. This was a totally real experience for Mother and she was excited and happy when she told us about it. As far as she was concerned Daddy had been in the room with her.

I called Daddy's brother Lenus in Oklahoma. He called Martin and Leslie in Wahoo, Nebraska. That weekend all three brothers were with us cheering us up, putting Mother in a private room at the hospital and seeing that our needs were met. Then big brother Paul came with Grandpa Jacobson from Illinois. These visits meant so much to Mother, sick as she was, and of course to us children.

We did realize that our parents were in grave jeopardy and that we could lose both of them. I can remember being anxious but was still confident that Mother would recover and that Daddy's ship would have a safe journey. And indeed the day came when we received a cablegram from Capetown which said only "Love, Ralph." He had arrived! I hastily drove to the hospital to personally deliver the wonderful news to Mother. We cried and laughed together. While I was there our good Dr. Knabb walked in and told me that Mother was out of danger. Our prayers were answered. A few days later I brought her home and she gathered each of the nine of us into her arms, one at a time of course.

"THE HEALTHIEST LARGE FAMILY IN GREENE COUNTY"

The public health department of our county, working with the schools, was conducting significant programs to promote and protect the health of children. Mother and Daddy realized their value and cooperated fully.

The Greene County health nurse, Mrs. Bertha Stevens, had a great impact and really made these programs come alive. She visited Blackman School several times a year and her coming was always a special occasion. She was a jolly, vivacious, motherly lady who seemed to enjoy us as much as we did her. She checked height, weight, posture, vision, hearing and examined our teeth and tonsils. Then she gave a demonstration-lecture to show us how to stay healthy. She skillfully manipulated a little hand-puppet named 'Monkey Joe' who had his own toothbrush, handkerchief, wash rag, towel, and spectacles. With these accessories she put him through his paces to demonstrate personal hygiene. She then showed us how the little monkey didn't even cry when he got his shots.

Dr. John Williams, the county health director, visited our school once or twice during the school year. He gave diphtheria and smallpox immunizations to those who needed them and whose parents had signed permission. Those were the only vaccines available for children at that time. Dr. Williams also checked the tonsils of those students about whom the nurse or the teacher was concerned. If the throat looked bad he would refer the child to his or her own private doctor for a tonsillectomy. In the pre-antibiotic era that operation was considered a valuable weapon against chronic tonsillitis and a possible way to reduce the incidence of rheumatic fever.

Efforts were made to encourage rural children to eat a more healthful diet. We Hult children went home for lunch because our house was only one hundred yards from school. Mother usually cooked a hot meal fortified with her delicious home-baked whole wheat bread. All the other students brought their lunches, which were carried in two-quart syrup pails.

A couple of families always brought only soda biscuits smeared with lard. Others had nothing but chunks of cornbread. The health department encouraged teachers to improvise some kind of a hot lunch once a week during the winter months. When this happened we Hults were given permission to stay at school during the noon hour. I remember Mrs. Highfill creating delicious stews on a little electric hot plate with meat which she brought and vegetables such as potatoes, onions and carrots which the students were encouraged to contribute. Each student brought his or her own dish or cup.

One goal of the program was to have each pupil receive a Nine-Point health award. Points were counted for smallpox and diphtheria vaccinations, a birth certificate, good teeth, normal tonsils, vision, hearing, posture and weight. In those days quite a few children were born at home without a doctor in attendance and no birth certification. With the parents' cooperation the health nurse and teacher helped to obtain this important document. When a throat looked bad the doctor would sometimes not issue the Nine-Point award until the student had a tonsillectomy. The same was true for dental care. I remember a friend who had to have his tonsils and adenoids out, several teeth pulled and others filled, in order to receive his health award. Students who passed the Nine-Point criteria five years in a row were given additional awards.

Each year an awards ceremony was conducted at the Greene County Rural Health Rally at a park in Springfield with attendance of up to 1000 students. I remember attending at least three of them. On April 25th, 1936, our parents took all eight of us, four blondes and four redheads, to the big event at Fassnight Park. Carl, 5, Martha, 3, and Gustav, 2, had received checkups and immunizations at a pre-school clinic and were given special awards. The buttons and certificates were given out to each teacher for distribution and special recognition was given to the students who had had to go through surgery or drastic dental care to achieve them. We were introduced as "probably the healthiest large family" at the event. A reporter for the Springfield News and Leader took our picture which appeared in the paper the next day. When the reporter interviewed him, Daddy had a hard time remembering our ages because, he said, "They change every year!" The big event was made more exciting by group games and refreshments and we all had a great time. If the rally had been scheduled ten days later the healthy family would have been even larger because on May 5th our youngest sister Mary was born.

Now sixty years later I am favorably impressed with the progressive and somewhat aggressive measures undertaken back then to promote the health of children. We have a lot more tools now but I'm not certain they are being applied as diligently as they were then, especially to the children who need help the most.

NOSTALGIC MEMORIES OF OUR PARENTS

This chapter consists of a collection of memories, musings, and anecdotes. They amplify my strong feeling that we were uniquely blessed growing up as a family with such dedicated loving Christian parents.

To me, Daddy was the most special man in the world. From my earliest memories he was stern but tender and loving. It was a great privilege as a small child to have him pick me up and hold me in his lap, but with such a multitude of younger brothers and sisters I was pretty much displaced at an early age. He still managed to find time for one-on-one contact with each of us. Arguments and fights between his children perplexed him sorely and he strongly emphasized the importance of family members truly caring for each other.

Each member of the family was cherished. Birthdays were always special occasions. With our limited resources we were encouraged to make birthday gifts for each other. Our sisters were more creative than the brothers. Paul and I would sometimes come up with such bright ideas as making a toy whistle or rabbit trap for each other. At the birth of a new brother or sister Daddy would plant a tree in honor of the new link in our family circle. Mother would always bake a cake and have a special meal in honor of the birthday boy or girl. Once she hid the frosted cake in the bedroom where toddler Gus was taking a nap. He awoke and made a wonderful mess of the cake and of himself.

In spite of the difficult times there was daily evidence of our parents' deep and romantic love for each other. They often took walks in the moonlight and we children were definitely not invited along. I remember overhearing Daddy talking lovingly to people outside our family about "my Gertrude." Only one time can I remember hearing them argue and it cut me to the quick. Daddy said something negative about Mother's housekeeping and she took offense. She argued that it was impossible to keep things neat with our large family in such limited space. I basically sympathized with Mother. If we showed any sign of disrespect or disobedience to Mother, Daddy's response was immediate and severe. On the many occasions he was away Mother looked forward to his letters and some of them were for her eyes alone. There was never any doubt in my mind about their deep love for each other.

Mutual sharing was a hallmark of the behavior code in our household. Both Mother and Daddy were careful to see that we shared and shared alike. On one occasion when there were 11 pieces of bacon for 10 of us. Daddy carefully cut the 11th piece into 10 parts and distributed one to each of us. If anything, when food was limited, they often took less than their own shares. In the 1930's Mother and Daddy were both underweight. Their children came first.

Discipline was stern but corporal punishment was reserved for the most serious infractions. I recall only once being spanked by Mother and that was with her bare hand. The four or five times Daddy punished me for serious offenses are recalled vividly. The instrument of correction was a 15-inch cane of rhinoceros hide which came from Africa. We referred to it with awe and apprehension as the 'kiboko,' the Swahili word for whip. Believe me, its administration made a lasting impression. After my deluge of tears Daddy would have tears in his own eyes as he explained why I had been punished.

One day the fragile old kiboko snapped in two while it was in action punishing one of us. Paul and I were definitely relieved at its demise. Furthermore it was never replaced. That was the last time Daddy physically chastised either of us. I somehow felt that Paul was the focal point of discipline more often than the rest of us. As the oldest brother more was expected of him. There was quite a storm when a pack of cigarettes was found in his pockets when he was 16. I think Daddy was more hurt than angry that his son would indulge in that horrible habit. All three of Daddy's brothers smoked and he was convinced that it was affecting their health.

Mother was a fine and resourceful cook, making our limited grocery bill go a long ways with nourishing meals. Daddy would buy a ten-cent soup bone. By adding whatever vegetables were in season, Mother would make a tasty stew. She had another trick to make a little food go a long way. She would take one or two eggs and add them to milk and flour in a frying pan. From this she would concoct a satisfying breakfast for all of us called 'eggarerra' in Swedish, which we ate as a gravy over toast. I like to think of it as poor man's scrambled eggs.

Mother's delicious homemade bread accounted for a significant percentage of our calorie intake. For breakfast we ate hot cereal made of corn or wheat meal ground by hand in a little mill turned by one of us children. Of course no breakfast was more appreciated than pancakes. Another vital part of our diet came from the fruit and vegetables which Mother canned by the hundreds of quarts. Our parents also saw to it that we drank plenty of milk. We looked forward to having a glass of buttermilk on churning day.

Mother was a natural athlete. Her brothers were proud of telling us that she had never lost a race in grade school and high school. One day when I was probably 11 years old she challenged me to a race from the barn to the house, a distance of about 50 yards. I thought it would be a snap to outrun my middle-aged Mom. (She was 36 years old.) She even gave me a head start and beat me by several yards. I didn't tell my friends anything about that little event.

She also had been a member of the Augustana College women's basketball team. Mother could hit, throw and catch a baseball as well as most boys. I remember vividly the time one of our roosters attacked 6-year-old Eunice, cutting her on the face with his spurs. Mother picked up a rock and hit him squarely on the head, knocking him unconscious. We had him for supper that night.

We nearly lost Carl for the second time when he was about two. A family friend had brought us some lemon drops which we children were all enjoying. Somebody said something to make little Carl laugh and he began choking uncontrollably. He rapidly became blue in the face and struggled desperately to breathe. We older children stood around helplessly not knowing what to do. Mother was in the kitchen and heard our hysterical reactions and Carl's awful choking. She ran into the room and without a moment's hesitation, grabbed an ankle with her left hand, suspended her husky toddler upside down and gave him a sharp whack on the back with her right hand. Out popped the lemon drop and within a minute a scared and crying little boy was pink again. If Mother hadn't been there and instinctively reacted, I'm afraid Carl wouldn't be with us today.

One of my favorite childhood recollections is of Daddy's coming out of the bedroom in the morning in his long underwear. He would turn on the radio and tune it to the Kansas City station which opened its morning broadcast with John Phillip Sousa marches. He would turn up the volume to awaken any sleepyheads and then start marching around the room in step with the music. Five or more of us kids would form a line in stairstep rank behind Daddy and march around the room. This would continue until the volume of laughter drowned out the sound of the radio.

Daddy never forgot his call to Africa. He liked to show us important places on a large wall map and was constantly looking for news and current information about the 'dark continent.' When the Ringling Brothers Circus came to Springfield he took Paul and me to see the performance. He especially wanted to see the Ubangi women from West Africa with their huge lip saucers. He knew they would be speaking French and introduced himself fluently in that language. He was soon surrounded and engaged in a noisy animated conversation. I remember how amazed the people around us were at the happy gabfest between Daddy and these exotic African women. The first commercial movie I recall seeing was "Trader Horn" about a famous English explorer and trader who did much to open up commerce in parts of Africa. Later our father escorted Paul and me to another movie on the life of Cecil Rhodes for whom the country of Rhodesia was named.

Daddy had a nice, quiet, somewhat subdued sense of humor. One of the times I remember him really laughing was during the visits of his youngest brother Lenus. Sometimes he was a little embarrassed at Mother's hearty pealing laughter. He did enjoy the things which made his children happy.

On one occasion I played a practical joke on him. One night he came home late, put the car in the barn, and shut the door. On the following morning before he got up I found a 7-foot blacksnake on the road which had just been run over by a car. I carefully placed it just behind our car so it would appear that Daddy had run over it the night before but didn't see it in the dark. I made sure to be on hand when he next opened the barn door. The moment he spotted the monstrous creature he jumped about 6 feet in the air. Very excitedly he returned to the house to have us come out and see the 'huge reptile' he had unwittingly run over the night before. He liked to tell the story to others and it seemed to me like the snake got a little bigger with each telling. During his lifetime I never admitted the prank to him; I did share it with my brother Paul.

During the depression Daddy pursued several avenues of generating income, including door-to-door sales of home products and books. Of course nobody had any money those days so he didn't make many sales. At one time we wondered if he could possibly get a job as a radio announcer. He certainly could have done a better job than some of the announcers we had in Springfield in those days. In 1933 he even went to work on a WPA road gang. We heard that his co-workers chided him for being too conscientious about putting in a full day's work.

Later he got a job doing grave restoration at the National Cemetery. In order to vote, one had to pay a poll tax in Greene County. As a good citizen Daddy worked off the poll tax by clearing the brush along county roads. He was definitely not afraid of physical labor. When working hard he sweated profusely. Ingrid and I remember his special aroma at the end of a day's work. Some people would call it B.O. but it wasn't offensive at all to us. It was uniquely his and he was so special to us that we had only pleasant associations with the odors he emanated.

Although Daddy was a strong Lutheran he had a good rapport with non-Lutheran Christians. Many of his good friends in the Ozarks were Baptists, and he frequently visited their Bible College in Springfield. He was hurt by the intolerance of the Missouri Synod Lutherans. On one occasion he was invited to speak on missions at Trinity Lutheran Church, but the pastor, Rev. Koerber, instructed Daddy specifically that he was not to utter a prayer. And he was never asked to conduct a Sunday morning worship service because Daddy's Augustana Synod was not doctrinally pure. Still he wanted us to be confirmed at Trinity because it was the only Lutheran church in Springfield. Paul, Ingrid and I were confirmed together on May 28th, 1939. We personally liked Rev. Koerber but there was always a certain resentment that our dear father wasn't considered a real pastor.

Until confirmation we children had Sunday School assignments at home. When we were prepared, Daddy would sit with us under a big oak tree in good weather and review the lesson with us. In this role he was more of a loving father than a stern teacher. Although he expected us to know our assignments, he was usually quite happy and relaxed during these sessions. On March 22, 1936, I made the following entry in my diary, "Daddy went to sleep while I was reciting my Sunday School lesson to him." I wasn't offended because I knew he was tired. I just enjoyed watching him sleep for a couple of minutes until his head dropped forward awakening him. That embarrassed him but it was an entirely pleasant memory for me.

As we got older there was more discussion of our adult roles. Daddy didn't get into any details of the birds and bees but said much about the wonder and beauty of the relationship between man and wife. I remember specifically that he told me it would make him happy if I found a nice Swedish girl.

Some of my most cherished memories come from the beginning and end of each day in our home in the Ozarks. At breakfast after Daddy had read a morning devotion we would join in prayer and sing, "Again Thy Glorious Sun Doth Rise." Even in the most trying times there was a strong theme of love, thanksgiving and optimism. Mother was particularly strong in looking on the bright side and finding the silver linings on our cloudy days.

In the evening after supper and homework, we would gather around the old reed organ and sing. Sometimes we sang familiar secular songs from "The Golden Book Of Favorite Songs," such as "Love's Old Sweet Song," "I'll Take You Home Again Kathleen," as well as patriotic or Stephen Foster songs. We would always end our song sessions with one or more favorite hymns such as "Day is Dying in The West," or "Children of the Heavenly Father." If there was a baby in our family circle, (and there usually was) we would sing as a lullaby, "Hush My Dear, Lie Still and Slumber." When I hear any of these hymns today, my memory screen flashes a picture of Mother seated at the organ with a gentle smile and Daddy looking fondly at her, then at each of us.

Evening Song Fest.

Study Time at home.

Confirmation. Backrow middle, Paul, John, Ingrid.

Gustav on guard in front of our one-holer! A fun example of Daddy's humor.

A DAY OF TRAGEDY AND SORROW

On January 2, 1932, the worst massacre of American law officers in a single incident occurred 11 miles west of our house. Six Greene County police officers were killed and three wounded by a pair of small-time criminals whom they had anticipated arresting without incident. I was only eight years old then but I can vividly remember the anguish and shock of our parents as the horrible news came over the radio. The whole county was plunged into deep anguish, mourning and anger.

I was not yet keeping a diary so my memories of those terrible days are limited. However, I recently discovered a book, "Young Brothers Massacre," written by Paul and Mary Barrett and published by the University of Missouri Press in 1988. This volume has graphically satisfied my curiosity about details unremembered.

By the turn of the century J.D. Young and his wife Willy had raised a family of 11 children in Missouri and Oklahoma. He was a hard-working farmer, highly respected in the community, upwardly mobile in establishing a prosperous future for his family. Originally he rented land in Christian County, Missouri, but saw his big chance in 1902, claiming a 160-acre homestead in former Indian Territory in Oklahoma. The family worked hard to build up the claim but were doomed by several years of drought. Still Mr. Young recovered $15,000 in selling the property. In those days that considerable fortune was enough to purchase a good farm back in Missouri. Further intensive effort enabled him to buy a much better property five miles west of Springfield in 1918, which became the site of the terrible events to come. After this fine man, who was a devout Baptist and tireless worker, died in 1921, the fortunes of the family went into decline. Some said he died of a broken heart as he watched three of his sons descend into a life of crime.

Eight of the siblings led exemplary and productive lives. Paul, the oldest of the notorious three, committed numerous burglaries and auto thefts in Missouri and Texas and was in and out of prison. Jennings and Harry, who mowed down the officers, followed in his footsteps. While he was alive, the father hired outstanding lawyers who saw to it that the three got minimal sentences. They were exempted from the WWI draft as farm laborers although they were reportedly highly allergic to work. In 1929, while being arrested for drunk and disorderly conduct, Harry shot and killed the city marshal of the small town of Republic. He escaped and eventually made good his vow to never be taken alive after his previous incarceration in the Missouri State Penitentiary.

The stage was set for the fateful day when two of the Young sisters tried to sell a car Harry had stolen in Texas to a Springfield auto dealer. He recognized the car as stolen and notified the city police who arrested the sisters. They called Sheriff Hendrix because the Young farm was in his jurisdiction. Together they rounded up a posse of ten deputies and Springfield police officers who drove in three cars to the Young farm. They seemed to think that their very numbers would scare whoever was holed up in the house into surrendering.

No significant cover protected the approaching lawmen. From their vantage point in the house, Harry and Jennings without warning mowed down nine of the ten officers with an automatic rifle and repeating shotgun. Five died immediately and the sixth soon after being brought to the hospital. The other three officers survived their wounds.

Jennings and Harry escaped and managed to travel all the way to Houston, Texas. On January 5th, three days after the massacre, a boarding house owner rented them a room and on the same day recognized their pictures in a newspaper. He alerted police who responded quickly and surrounded the house. When the brothers realized that were hopelessly trapped they turned their guns on themselves. The mother and sisters were cleared of active involvement and were released. In addition to their private grief they suffered a terrible community-wide stigma. Paul was not implicated in the massacre but continued a life of crime for the next five years. He then went 'straight' and lived peacefully into his nineties.

Private funerals were held for each of the officers. On the following Sunday the Springfield American Legion held a public memorial service at the Landers Theater. The 1500-seat auditorium was filled with the crowd overflowing out into the street. Daddy took Paul and me and we were able to find seats near the back. Missouri Governor Caulfield was the principal speaker. I don't remember the contents of his address, but it was a somber emotionally charged event. I do recall distinctly that our Dad held my hand at least part of the time during the service.

The Ozarks region had more than its share of notorious criminals. Much of the crime was at least partly attributed to desperate poverty. Harold Bell Wright had immortalized the infamous Bald Knobbers Gang in his book, "Shepherd Of The Hills." The legendary exploits of Pretty Boy Floyd took on something of a Robin Hood flavor when he allegedly gave some of the loot from bank robberies to poor people. We heard unconfirmed reports that he had some association with the Young brothers. Jake Fleagle, a vicious bank robber and murderer, was killed by law officers two years before the Young massacre not 30 miles away in Verona. I have previously written about Daddy's dangerous encounter with him at our house 24 hours before Jake was shot down. Bonny and Clyde also committed some of their crimes in the Ozarks.

We boys were very much aware of all of these notorious characters and attempted to recreate with carved wooden weapons their dastardly deeds in our games of cops-and-robbers. The Young massacre gave us fresh material, but we tended then to set the stage so the good guys came out on top. At that age I couldn't quite appreciate our parents' intense aversion to such play. Now as a parent and grandparent I'm horrified to see children doing the same thing with space-age weapons. Unfortunately man's inhumanity to man has roots in early childhood, and we keep making the same mistakes over and over again.

CREATURES GREAT AND SMALL

Many hours of my childhood were spent watching, listening to, and marveling at the fascinating inhabitants of the world around me. While engaged in such endeavors I was totally oblivious to anything else. One day Daddy became exasperated with me when I was supposed to be picking apples. He found me lying on my tummy under the apple tree fully absorbed in studying the activities of a busy ant colony. He must have watched me patiently for a minute or so before he commented that my daily quota of fruit-picking was far from being fulfilled. If he hadn't come along I might have been there for an hour, mesmerized by all the comings and goings of the tiny creatures.

Birds were high on my list as subjects for observation, and robins were my favorite birds. Every spring I was thrilled when the first robins appeared and began singing their hearts out as they staked out their territories. I watched carefully to see where they built their nests and tried to find concealed observation points near the nests where I could make daily inspections to see how the adults were progressing with their parental responsibilities. Then I would report my findings to the family at mealtime. For example, "The mother robin laid the fourth egg today." or, "The first baby hatched today!" When I was about six years old a pair of robins nested six feet up in one of our larger apple trees. The adjacent tree had a wonderful observation post where I could stealthily climb up and look down into the nest. When I first discovered the nest it contained four beautiful sky blue eggs. After they hatched I made daily rounds to watch the parents diligently feeding their babies. When the four babies were half grown I made one of my daily inspection visits. As I neared the tree I heard the parents angrily scolding and saw them flying around the nest. I climbed to my observation post and was horrified to see a huge black snake wrapped around the trunk of the tree at the level of the nest. It was just swallowing the last of the babies. I was broken-hearted and burst into tears. At that age I was genuinely afraid of snakes so did not go after the murderer. Instead I hurried home weeping all the way and shared my sorrow with Mother. She was good at consoling little boys but I still had difficulty going to sleep that night. Not long thereafter I caught a blue jay raiding a robin's nest of tiny babies and had another villain to add to my list.

Another common bird at Bethany Homestead was a delicate creature with a wonderful song which we called a ground sparrow. Members of this species concealed their nests in ground-level foliage. Every year I found a number of their nests and watched them raise their families. On several occasions I found oversized eggs in ground sparrow nests laid by cowbirds. These lazy birds rely on other parents to incubate and raise their offspring. When I found these big eggs in the wrong nests I removed them. Somebody reminded me that it was futile to mess with Mother Nature but I just couldn't see such an injustice without taking what action I could.

My favorite bird song was that of the mockingbird which could accurately imitate the call of almost all other birds. We even had one who liked to duplicate the sound of our telephone ringing. Our region was well populated with Bob White quails. Paul and I liked to imitate their unique calls and get them to answer us. The call of Canadian geese flying north in spring and south in fall was a nostalgic reminder of the changing seasons.

As much as I enjoyed birds I spent even more time watching, marveling at, and sometimes being amused by the antics and intricate lifestyles of the insect world.

In the dry heat of summer I noticed a number of two-inch inverted cone-shaped depressions in the dust around our house. I asked Paul what had caused them and he said each of them had been made by an "ant lion." As a demonstration he caught an ant and dropped it into one of those little excavations. Immediately there were little flicks of dirt shooting up from the bottom of the hole which trapped the ant and kept it from climbing out. Then a pair of vicious looking pincers reached up, grasped the ant and pulled it under the surface as if it were sinking into quicksand. Paul then dug up the cone and showed me an ugly half-inch larva which was devouring the ant. "That," he explained. "is an ant lion!" The mother, an insect which looks like a dragon fly, had laid an egg which hatched into this creature which excavated the trap in which to catch his food. After transforming into an adult, it mates and starts another generation. This lifestyle wasn't very favorable for the poor ants but what a marvelously ingenious setup for the baby ant lions. Later on I believe I demonstrated this remarkable setup to my little brothers, Carl, Gus, and David.

Another more amusing natural drama which I never tired of watching as a small boy was provided by dung beetles. When a mating pair of these half-inch shiny black beetles discovered a pile of fresh cow manure they immediately set to work. They carved a gum-ball sized chunk out of the cow patty. With one pushing and the other pulling they started rolling their prize away, struggling uphill and then comically rolling downhill. When they found a suitable site they excavated a hole into the ground large enough to accommodate their dung ball. It took much effort to bury their treasure in the hard clay soil. What I didn't know was that the female dung beetle laid an egg on the dung ball. Later this hatched and grew into a fat larva feeding on this nutritious mass. Three decades later I had the privilege of watching an even more impressive demonstration of dung beetle diligence. On a hunting trek in Tanzania we came across a writhing mass of huge dung beetles making short work of a bushel basket sized pile of fresh elephant droppings.

Another wildlife drama which I observed many times concerned the lifestyle of mud-daubers which were beautiful little blue black wasps. They flew to the edge of our pond or any convenient puddle and rolled up chunks of mud with which they molded coffin-shaped clay chambers under the eaves of our buildings. These were impervious to bird and insect predators. One day I watched a mud-dauber chasing a spider which it attacked and stung. In a few moments the spider was immobilized, the wasp picked it up and flew away. I presumed that this was lunch for the adult wasp. Later I broke open an apparently abandoned mud-dauber nest. I discovered that each chamber contained one or more paralyzed spiders and a single wasp larva which was feeding on them.

Spiders were fascinating subjects for my nature studies too. I spent many minutes watching spiders weave their beautiful webs and then capture the unwary insects which flew into them, including mud-daubers, so the predator can sometimes become the victim. Trapdoor spiders dig a hole in the ground and surround the opening with a fine web which functions like a telegraph wire network. When an insect lands on this web the spider rushes out to capture it. Before I was old enough to know better I stuck my index finger into a trapdoor hole and felt a sharp pain. When I reflexly jerked it out, a fat brown spider was attached to the tip my finger. Fortunately she didn't inject too much venom but the pain lasted for an hour and was every bit as intense as a bee sting. I never again repeated that experiment.

Much of the United States east of the Rocky Mountains is populated with a charming little nocturnal bug. We children looked forward each summer to the nightly display of fireflies, otherwise called lightning bugs. We were awed by their ability to turn their little lanterns off and on and sparkle the evening away. Mother explained that their bodies contained special chemicals which they could mysteriously control with their little brains. She indicated that they used this display to attract mates and to entertain little boys and girls. When I first caught one I noticed that the whole abdominal section lit up with a lovely yellow-green glow about every six seconds. I couldn't feel any warmth and wondered why the little body didn't get hot. Paul and I discovered that we could rub their bodies on our faces and make streaks of Indian "war paint." Mother discouraged this practice because it destroyed the beautiful little creatures. We liked to catch a number of fireflies and put them into jars. If I captured enough of them the light produced by their little bodies was enough to read by. I tried putting a whole jarful of them on my bedside table and could actually read a book with the natural illumination which was about as bright as a small candle. Firefly larvae give off a faint fluorescent light and are sometimes called glowworms. In Europe there is a wingless species in which the adult females light up intensely. They are probably the inspiration for the enchanting song, "Glow, little glowworm, glimmer, glimmer!" Children aren't the only humans astounded by lightning bugs. Our Oregon-raised son-in-law couldn't believe his eyes when he first saw them two years ago on a trip to the Midwest. I think that discovery was one of the high points of his trip.

Another indelible auditory memory of my childhood was produced by cicadas, otherwise known as 17-year locusts. These spectacular 2-inch insects sport bright green bullet-shaped bodies with red eyes and lacy transparent wings. The mating call of the males is a noisy but haunting buzzing sound which is somewhat similar to the oscillating noise of a modern emergency vehicle. When multiplied many times by hundreds of competing males the sound is truly deafening. One day I watched a large ugly brown insect crawling up a tree trunk. I was mesmerized to see its back crack open and a beautiful green adult cicada slowly emerge. The original tan skin was left hanging on the tree. A few moments later a blue jay swooped down and carried away my pet locust before he could fulfill his life's destiny.

I had difficulty believing that the larvae and nymph stages of cicadas lasted 17 years but entomologists insist that such is the case. When a female locates her noisy amorous boy friend they mate and she lays her eggs in small living twigs. When the eggs hatch, the larvae damage the twigs which fall to the ground. The larvae tunnel several inches into the ground and undergo their 17-year infancy and adolescence. One cicada species has a 13-year cycle. We noticed that during some summers there were far more cicadas singing their love songs than others. That meant that living conditions had been more favorable for reproduction with less predation 17 years earlier. I had difficulty believing that these beautiful little bugs were much older than I was.

A true harbinger of spring in the Ozarks was the onset of the mating calls of frogs and toads. A veritable symphony of medium pitched music came from the leopard frogs in our pond 100 yards from the house counter-pointed by the deep bass "jug-o-rum" from the less numerous bullfrogs. Tree frogs or peepers warbled their high-pitched arias from shrubs and trees near the house.

Many times I fell asleep to the lullaby of this wonderful soothing music.

Mother needed a storage place for the hundreds of jars of fruit and vegetables which she canned. To this end Daddy decided to dig and construct a cellar about 75 yards south of the house. When his 8 x10-foot hole was three feet deep he ran into a limestone ledge. He had to use dynamite to penetrate this obstacle. Beneath the limestone was a shallow cave, the floor of which was made up of clay. Daddy went on to dig the hole about five feet deep, built steps, covered it with railroad ties and clay and constructed storage shelves. We were proud of his completion of this storage facility which could have doubled as a tornado shelter. Fortunately we never had to use it for the latter purpose. Soon after it was completed and stocked, Mother asked me to go fetch a jar of blackberries. They were stored on a shelf right next to the little cave underneath the limestone ledge. In the light of my flashlight I reached for the blackberries and was shocked to see a monster in the cave the likes of which I had never seen. It was six inches long, and shiny black with orange spots. I had recently read about poisonous Gila monsters and wondered if this could be a similar dangerous creature. I grabbed a jar of blackberries and hurried back into the house. Daddy came out with me and identified my discovery as a harmless salamander or mud puppy.

Soon after that Paul and I were swimming in our pond and noticed some very strange looking tadpoles, much longer than those whose parents were frogs. They had round heads and long narrow bodies. We even thought they might be catfish but didn't see how fish could have reached our pond. Then we spotted a black and orange salamander swimming out of the little cave at the head of the pond. As we followed the progress of the strange tadpoles they sprouted legs and the tails became longer. They were obviously salamanders. We learned some amazing facts. Salamanders can grow a new leg or tail if such members are amputated. Some species can actually change their sex from male to female and back again.

When threatened, salamanders secrete a toxic white substance from the skin of their backs which discourages predators. They share this characteristic with some of their toad cousins and poisonous South American tree frogs

These are just a few of the creature friends and associates of my childhood. Their fascinating foibles definitely prevented major boredom in my young life. And they helped to convince me that there was a great Creator responsible for their very existence and for the entire universe of which we humans are a part.

"DEAR DIARY" (1935-1938)

My parents gave me my first diary as a Christmas gift in 1934. Daddy suggested that in years to come I would appreciate looking back and reliving the adventures of my childhood. He was correct. Mother encouraged me to record the events that were most important to me in my daily life. That's exactly what I did, but today I wish that I had written more subjective information about how I felt about what was happening around me and inside of me. That didn't happen because I was fearful of submitting my true feelings in a form accessible to the secret scrutiny of my big brother and my sisters.

My 1935 diary begins with a panel of identification data indicating name, address, and phone number (63F13). My age was ten and a half years, my weight eighty-six pounds and my height four feet and nine inches. Hair color is recorded as "dark red" and eye color "blue." The first entry on Jan.1 reads, "We began the new year by singing a little song and greeting it as pleasantly as we could. Had weather bright and fair, just the kind anybody would want to begin the New Year. Had a pleasant day at school."

This was the first of my 1455 daily inscriptions through Dec. 31, 1938. If you are mathematically inclined you will notice that number is six days short of four years plus one extra day for Leap Year. The 1938 diary is missing one page for the days of Dec. 14-19. On Dec 20 I wrote, "Page lost, but nothing much happened."

The truth of the matter was that in a moment of weakness I had written something about a girl upon whom I had a powerful crush. Soon thereafter I realized that for obvious reasons this had better not be a part of my permanent record. I would have been terribly embarrassed if my older brother or sisters had read it so I tore out the page and burned it.

For the first two years, all of my entries were carefully recorded in ink with a fountain pen. By 1937 I became more casual and started using a lead pencil part of the time.

Almost every day I included a weather report which often indicated the presence or absence of clouds, temperature, and precipitation figures. Concern and anxiety were often reflected during the drought years of 1935 and 1936. I recorded the dust clouds moving in from the southwest from the dust bowl areas of Oklahoma with the following entry:

March 1, 1935. There was a thick cloud of dust hanging over all day. Dust covered everything. Cars even left new tracks in the layer of dust on the gravel road.

The lines in my diary bring back a flood of other memories including the gritty teeth, brown discoloration of sweaty skin, the terrible time Mother had keeping the house and clothes clean, and bees raising little clouds of dust as they made their rounds of the apple blossoms.

The following selected quotes will indicate a few of the events which were important to me during those four years. Family birthdays and anniversaries were recorded. The vital statistics of our livestock population took up considerable space in my journals. Opportunities to work for neighbors and earn welcome extra cash were faithfully reported. Occasionally news bulletins from the realms of politics, sports and current events crept into my daily writings.

1935

Jan. 4: Congress met to make new laws. Heard President Roosevelt give message on a nationwide hook-up.

Jan. 9: Poor old Uncle Lund died today. (Rev. C. O. Lund had inspired Daddy to go into the ministry.)

Jan. 11: Amelia Earhart attempts flight across the Pacific.

Jan. 17: We played tackle at school and had a lot of fun.

Jan. 21: School was canceled because of the record cold. (Minus 2 degrees F.) Paul and I had to sleep in the house because it was too cold in the boys' cottage.

Jan. 27: We went skating on the pond. I tore my new Christmas overalls from hip to ankle while climbing over a fence. (I brought them to Mama with tears in my eyes and she immediately sewed them as good as new on her sewing machine.)

Feb. 1: I finished my first month sweeping the schoolhouse (My first real job for which I was paid the princely wages of $2.50 per month.)

Feb. 3: Today was the day for the sun eclipse. We watched it.

Feb. 10: The weather looked bad this morning but all of a sudden the sun peeped through the clouds and it was warm and fair the rest of the day.

Feb. 11: Today was Thomas A. Edison's birthday.

Feb. 13: Eunice broke out with German measles.

Feb. 18: I received information in the mail on the state of Missouri, which I had sent for last week for my history report.

Mar. 6: Oliver Wendell Holmes of the Supreme Court died today.

Mar. 8: Little Martha and Gustav had their diphtheria inoculations at school today. (The rest of us had already had them.)

Mar. 11: It rained all day. The pond started to run over and all the little valleys were filled with raging torrents. The James River valley was a vast mass of moving water from a rain which almost broke the previous record.

Mar. 16: There was a heavy cloud of dust from the southwest. We have flooding while Oklahoma is suffering from the dust storm.

Mar. 21: We got a new broom at school today and I got through sweeping in half the usual time.

Mar. 25: We got a little bull calf from the old cow. It was quite a disappointment because we expected a heifer.

Mar. 30: We planted our first potatoes today. We also ate some spinach from the garden that we had planted last fall.

Apr. 1: Mr. Claytor's dog died today. He felt so bad about it.

Apr. 9: We set the electric incubator with 48 eggs and plan to set a hen too.

Apr. 16: Today was the beginning of baseball season.

Apr. 18: We gave the operetta Aunt Drusilla's Garden in the evening. Poor Mrs. Highfill broke down and cried because she won't be with us next year. She gave out the grade cards and I passed into the 7th grade.

Apr. 19: Today was the last day of school. We had a picnic down near the creek. We toasted weenies and marshmallows and had a lot of fun. (Children today would envy us if they knew that our school year ended in April.) Mama was elected president of the PTA.

Apr. 20: There are four wild ducks on our pond.

Apr. 24: I picked up 100 pails of rocks from the garden this morning. (Each time the soil was plowed a new crop of rocks appeared.)

Apr. 27: Today was the county rural health day. A newspaper photographer took my picture with refreshments he bought for me. (The Green County Health Rally was a 'fun and games' day for all the rural students who had participated in the health screening and immunization program. I didn't have any spending money and the photographer must have seen me enviously watching my friends buying goodies at the refreshment stand. He asked me if he could take my picture if he bought me a coke and a popsicle. He didn't have to wait for a response. I couldn't believe my good fortune!)

Apr. 29: Paul and I worked for Larimers, pulling weeds and hoeing from 8:00 until noon. For those four hours we got twenty cents each---enough to buy five-year health awards for Ingrid, Paul, and me. (These were little certificates and pin-on buttons of which we were very proud).

Apr. 30: An aeroplane wrote "PHILLIPS 66" in the sky. (For us, this was an astounding feat in 1935.)

May 3: Our garden is doing fine. The potatoes are coming up good. We expect frost tomorrow.

May 4: Thanks to God we didn't have frost. Today was the 61st Kentucky Derby.

May 5: Daddy went down and milked in Paul's place at Creightons. (13-year-old Paul had a regular job milking for these neighbors and Daddy apparently felt that his son needed a break to catch up on his sleep.)

May 6: Dizzy Dean fanned Babe Ruth and hit a home run himself. (This was an exhibition game between the St. Louis Cardinals and the New York Yankees. Babe Ruth was in the twilight of his career.)

May 7: Paul and I played horseshoes after we got all of our chores done. (We used the shoes which the horses had worn out. Throwing a ringer was considered a major miracle.)

May 8: Daddy brought a man home for dinner. His last name is Erickson and he says that he is a direct descendant of Lief Erickson. (I believe our parents were skeptical about that claim. He was quite a talker.) We also took the old cow to the neighbor's bull today.

May 11: Daddy went to town and bought 6,000 onion plants and 90 Wyandotte chicks.

May 12 We got a little heifer calf from the young cow today. She is quite like her mother and today is-s-s Mother's Day. (I didn't write anything about what we did for Mother Gertrude but I'm sure we didn't forget her.)

May 13: Paul and I planted 1,000 onion plants today.

May 16: Daddy sold the bull calf and got 10 dollars. He weighed 140 pounds. (The weight must have been referring to the calf because Daddy weighed more than that. At any rate ten dollars was a princely sum at our house in 1935.)

May 18: Paul went with Mamma and Daddy to the county 8th grade commencement exercises and got his diploma. It sure was a big day for him! I had to stay home with the rest of the bunch and it wasn't such an easy matter! [The 'rest of the bunch' consisted of Gustav (13 months), Martha (3), Carl (4½), Eunice (6), Veda (7½), and Ingrid (9). At that time my age was 10 years and 11 months. In this day and age people would be horrified at the tender age of the senior baby sitter, but we were expected to take responsibility early. And I must admit that although she was two years younger, my sister Ingrid was more mature and much more of a 'take charge' person than I was. She was usually the one who had to change Gus' diapers. I should indicate too that we did have a telephone and could have called neighbors in case of emergency. Another factor which made the experience less painful was the reality that we were all pretty fond of each other, and we were committed to the proposition that we'd have a good report for our parents when they came home.]

May 28: Today was the Dionne quintuplets' first birthday. There was quite a celebration. They are the first quintuplets to live over 14 days. (I remember discussing with my brother Paul what our situation would be like if, instead of having Baby Gus, Mother had borne quintuplets.)

May 30: Today was Memorial Day.---We had the young cow bred again. (We weren't very imaginative. At that point our two dairy animals were 'the old cow' and 'the young cow.')

June 3: Daddy worked at his desk all day. Paul and I worked on the yard. I hauled 6 big carts of rocks and Paul cut all the weeds.

June 5: Daddy went to Rock Island to attend Cousin Oscar's ordination as a Pastor. He rode with a truck driver to save money. We had the old cow bred at Creightons.

June 12: We found a scorpion. It is quite unusual for this part of the country.

June 13: I found a tarantula spider as big as my hand under a limestone rock (I captured it in a pint jar and it lived for several days. I didn't know what to feed it.)

June 17: We got a horse today. She is a sorrel mare and quite thin. We doctored our sick pig. Today is Mama and Daddy's engagement anniversary. (How's that for covering the full spectrum of the daily news?)

June 18: We got some dewberries out of the orchard. We named our horse Dolly.

June 19: I worked at the wood and cut my finger to the bone. (Mamma wrapped it up snugly and it healed as neatly as it would have with stitches.)

June 20: Mamma and Daddy took the little children to a preschool clinic at Brookline.

June 21: I had quite a nice birthday. (My eleventh) We had the young cow bred today. (That was the third time in three months. We apparently had a bovine infertility problem.)

June 24: We got word that Grandma Hult and her sister Great Aunt Ida Lund with three of their children, are coming in two days.

June 26: Our folks came in the evening. It sure was nice to reunite with them.

June 27: Eunice sure had a nice birthday with all the folks here. Cousin Bennie took Paul and me to town and bought us a baseball and some firecrackers. (Our second cousin Ben Lund was then a medical student at the University of Minnesota and became a lifelong friend.) In the evening we had a picnic at the fish hatchery.

June 28: We joined a 4-H calf club today and found it quite interesting. (This was our introduction to 4-H club activities which were to play an important role in widening our horizons over the following six years.)

July 3: Paul and I picked up 35 bushels of apples today. We have picked up 108 bushels in the last ten days. (These were second grade apples which were used to make vinegar and feed the livestock.)

Healthy and Happy!
Photo in *Springfield Leader and Press*.

July 4: Today is the glorious old Fourth. We tried to sell some apples today. (Paul and I set up a little stand by the road where cars passed on their way to the James River. We were asking 25 cents per bushel but didn't make a single sale!)

July 9: Today is Daddy's 47th birthday. It is also his and Mamma's 16th wedding anniversary.

July 11: Today is Sister Ruth's birthday. She died the same day she was born. (She was born in Tanganyika in 1923. Mother said that she was a plump healthy little girl and felt that the British nurse didn't wrap her up warmly enough so that she got chilled.

Then Mother said that if Ruth had lived they wouldn't have had me in 1924. She went on to declare that if they had later had a little boy named John he would have been a totally different person than I was. I didn't know whether that was supposed to make me feel good or bad, but knowing Mother, I leaned toward accepting it as a compliment.)

This has become a rather prolonged potpourri of my diary entries of 1935. Quite a bit of family history transpired. There will be further elaboration on some of the events in subsequent stories.

ONE-HORSE FARMING

Much of Bethany Homestead's thirty-eight acres was occupied by the orchard so there was only a small area available for other agricultural pursuits. Our parents planned to be as self-sustaining as possible which meant that we would raise much of our own food. To feed our large family we planted huge gardens with just about every vegetable which would grow in the Ozarks.

Daddy decided that we should have a relatively large poultry operation to produce enough eggs to sell in Springfield for a year-round cash flow. Then we needed a few cows, pigs, and goats for meat and milk. We children had a special affection for our livestock which made them a big part of our daily lives. Tears would flow when an animal died or was sold. There was much excitement when a new animal was born or a set of chicks hatched in our incubator.

We also had pets who played important roles in our lives at Bethany Homestead. Soon after we moved to Springfield the previous owner gave us a handsome young male German Shepherd named Von. He was allegedly purebred but it was too much of a hassle and expense to get registration papers. He immediately attached himself to Paul, apparently thinking that our big brother was the dominant male to whom he should show absolute affection and allegiance. Von tolerated the rest of us but he and Paul were inseparable. With his powerful bark and formidable appearance he made a fine watchdog. After he had been a part of our lives for about five years he became quite ill. Paul was devastated when Von died and carefully buried him in the shade of a special apple tree where the dog liked to rest. That was one of the few times I can remember seeing my big brother in tears. Von was soon replaced by a stub-tailed part-Airedale mutt named Pal. This medium-sized affectionate pooch was much loved by all of us. Pal seemed to feel that he had a proprietary responsibility to look out for the youngest members of our family. He was a special part of our family for years. We also kept one or two cats who pretty much looked out for themselves. They received an abundance of affection and attention from my younger brothers and sisters. They always hung around when we were milking and we enjoyed squirting milk into their mouths.

At no time did we have more than one horse. I can remember three of them over our thirteen years on Bethany Homestead. The first was named 'Dokey' after the Fulani word for 'iron horse' which Daddy had learned in his days in West Africa. This skinny old sorrel gelding definitely had a mind of his own. If he didn't feel like pulling the plow, a great deal of verbal (and some physical) admonishment was required to get him to move. I remember moments of total exasperation on Daddy's part when he would revert to some angry Swedish expletives which I didn't understand. I'm certain they weren't complimentary but they seemed to be more effective than English in getting Dokey to head up the field. Perhaps the old nag understood Swedish or more likely recognized his master's frame of mind when he resorted to that language. He was a little more cooperative when hitched to a cart or implement with wheels. I remember the happier moments of going into the barn with its pleasant horsey odor to bring Dokey an apple. He expressed his appreciation with a muffled whinny and let me caress the soft skin over his muzzle. He also enjoyed being curried at the end of a day's labor.

None of us rode any of our three horses often. Their sharp backbones weren't conducive to comfort and we didn't have a saddle. Still, the younger brothers and sisters enjoyed an occasional session way up high with somebody alongside to keep them from falling.

By the age of twelve I reached a special developmental landmark when I learned to plow. Much pride and satisfaction arose from plodding along behind the horse with the reins around my waist and being able to hold the handles steady. A cascade of black earth rolled up over the shiny plowshare sometimes revealing unexpected treasure such as a beautiful rock, an Indian arrowhead, or a fat earthworm to save for fishing. At the end of the furrow I enjoyed looking back to watch the birds foraging in the freshly turned soil. Unfortunately, in our rocky soil there were many bumps, grinds, stops and starts. You had to be careful to prevent the plow handles from flying up and jolting you in the ribs. Finishing the final furrow at the center of the field at day's end brought a special aura of accomplishment and satisfaction.

We started with one cow when we first moved to Springfield and slowly built the 'herd' up to a maximum of five. Mother had a special affection for cattle and did most of the milking until Paul and I developed our squeezing muscles. At age ten I was judged old enough to give it a try. I sat on the one legged stool with my legs under the cow to form a tripod, grabbed two mammary appendages and squeezed. At first very little milk dribbled into the ten-quart pail between my knees, but gradually I became more accomplished. Milking became my favorite chore and there was considerable satisfaction in rhythmically filling the bucket topped with a nice head of foam. This time also afforded a good opportunity for practicing my school recitations, singing, or just daydreaming. On cold winter mornings it was nice to warm my hands and nestle my forehead head against the cow's steaming flank. I had to be careful because cows, like humans, don't like intimate contact with icy fingers. In summer there was the hazard of being whacked on the head with a powerful tail as its owner tried to chase away the flies. We had one cow who kicked viciously and had to be hobbled with a chain device during milking.

Carl Harrowing

GROWING UP IN THE OZARKS / 79

Our Dairy Herd

Eunice and Martha

Paul, Gus, Carl and me with our dog Von

Feeding the chickens in front of our barn/garage/library

In hot weather we often milked outdoors with the cow's head chained to a metal fence. One evening I was thus occupied when a sudden storm approached with thunder rumbling and lightning flashing. I saw a bolt strike a tree next to our fence about a hundred yards away. At the same instant I was nearly knocked off the stool by a shock of electricity into my arms. It apparently came through the fence, through the chain, through the cow and into the two teats to which my hands were at that moment attached. The frightened animal jumped and kicked the bucket from between my legs, spilling the milk. I hurriedly released her from the fence, led her into the barn and finished my chore. Fortunately the lightning struck far enough away to minimize the damage. Had it been closer there might have been a 'shocking' demise of both milker and milkee.

As our little dairy operation expanded there was a surplus of milk. Daddy purchased a used centrifugal cream separator. We children were astounded as we watched fresh milk flowing from above being transformed into a trickle of thick cream from one spout and a larger stream of skim milk from the other. A fair amount of muscle was required to turn the big crank which rotated the centrifuge at high speed. Initially Paul was the only one of us kids able to 'grind the milk' as one of the younger siblings labeled the operation. I was thrilled when I became strong enough to turn the big handle. It was much more exciting to perform this feat of magic than to help wash dishes. After a while separating became less appealing and we were more than ready to relinquish this privilege to a younger brother or sister who proudly took over.

Churning butter from cream was another chore which had a certain fascination. We had a glass churn which held up to two quarts of cream. Four wooden blades rotated horizontally as a small crank was turned vertically on the side. This took far less manpower than separating but more patience. Sometimes it seemed to take forever. It was exciting to see the first little yellow flecks gradually coalesce into big globs of butter. There was a singular satisfaction and culinary delight in spreading a slice of Mother's delicious home-baked bread with butter you had churned yourself.

As the depression deepened we desperately needed cash so we were introduced to a new inexpensive white butter substitute called oleomargarine. Our cream was sold to Swift Produce Company in Springfield and we started using oleo. The dairy lobby in Washington D.C. mandated that it couldn't be colored to imitate butter but permitted the customer to color it at home with a little packet of orange coloring enclosed in the package. We agreed that it was better than nothing, but it certainly didn't taste like butter.

During the 1930's the federal government tested cattle for tuberculosis and Bang's disease, otherwise known as brucellosis. Two men checked out our cows by doing a skin test at the base of the tail. That wasn't so bad but I was horrified when they took out big syringes with huge needles. They proceeded to withdraw a large tube of blood from the jugular vein of each of our cows. Two days later they checked the skin tests which were all negative. In two weeks we got the report that our favorite cow, Belle, had Bang's disease and would have to be destroyed. We had no choice but to accept the $25 government check and let them remove her. She had miscarried twice so the test must have been accurate. Mother was especially saddened by this loss and I believe we all shed a few tears the day they hauled Belle away. She was a gentle creature who had provided us with over five gallons of milk per day for several years. We were actually fortunate that none of us was infected with brucellosis by drinking her unpasteurized milk.

THE JOHNSON GRASS BLUES

In summertime Ozark farmers lived in fear of a life-threatening hazard to their cattle, namely Johnson grass. This hardy drought-resistant perennial plant, had probably been imported from Africa. It showed promise as a hay crop, much like its close relative Sudan grass, but there were some serious drawbacks. First, it wasn't about to settle for just one year's growth. It sought to create its own brand of immortality by sending out tough underground runners in all directions. These swept around and choked out any other competing plant life and seemed to keep on growing even during the winter months. There were no herbicides available during those years so we spent many frustrating and backbreaking hours trying to hoe out the patches of Johnson grass invading other crops. Farmers with this aggressive weed in their fields weren't popular with their neighbors.

Even worse than the invasiveness was the potential of Johnson grass to produce a lethal poison for cattle. In dry hot weather, and right after the first frost, accumulations of prussic acid built up on the leaves and stalks. When this is consumed by the cattle, large amounts of gas are released into the intestinal tract and the victim suffocates because of pressure on the lungs. If discovered early enough, cattle can be saved by surgically puncturing the intestines and releasing the pressure.

One of the drought years of the 1930's was particularly bad for prussic acid poisoning. Pastures became dry and brown but Johnson grass with its deep roots remained green and inviting to the hungry cattle. They would often break down fences to reach it. Our next-door neighbors, the Creightons, went out to retrieve their cattle for milking one evening. They were devastated when they found that seven of their best dairy animals had broken through a fence and were lying dead in a field containing Johnson grass. That represented over half of their milk production at an already desperate time. Many other farmers in our region lost animals that year.

We were not spared at Bethany Homestead but didn't lose any of our milk cows. We were raising a bull calf to veal size to be sold at the stockyard for much needed cash. He was a happy frisky little fellow who received a lot of attention and affection from Paul and me. Early on we had weaned him from his mother and hand fed him from a pail of milk. As he got larger I enjoyed the excitement of mischievously grabbing his tail and having him tow me as fast as he could run around the pasture. That could probably be categorized as cruelty to animals but he didn't seem to mind. One sad day when he weighed about two hundred pounds and was just about ready for market he slipped through the fence and consumed a Johnson grass lunch. When we found him he was unconscious, lying on his side and barely breathing. Clearly he was dying before our eyes.

We were all in great distress. We children considered that little animal as one of our playmates. Daddy exclaimed, "What a loss! We needed that money so badly!" But Mother saw it differently and emphatically pronounced, "We are not going to let that meat go to waste!" She already knew that this type of animal poisoning did not affect the edibility of the meat if it was properly cooked. Mother promptly took charge of the situation like a general on a battlefield. First she ran into the kitchen and hurried back with a butcher knife in her right hand. We gaped with awe and horror as she ended the poor calf's misery by slashing his throat.

At that time we didn't have a refrigerator, not even an icebox. So Mother then issued an order to Daddy to put a washtub in the car and hurry to Springfield to purchase one hundred pounds of ice and a supply of one-pint Mason canning jars and lids. While he was gone she proceeded to skin and butcher the carcass. She must have had experience along these lines in her girlhood on the farm because she seemed to know what she was doing. By the time Daddy returned, our fatted calf had been reduced to manageable sized chunks which were packed in ice.

Mother then got out her pressure cooker which she filled with pint jars packed full with chunks of meat. This was fired up on the old wood stove in the sweltering heat of the kitchen for the prescribed number of minutes. I don't know how many times this operation was repeated but Mother was up much of the night. Within twenty-four hours she had canned over fifty pints of safe high quality animal protein to feed her family in the months ahead. She would take one jar of meat, add onions, tomatoes, carrots, turnips, potatoes, parsnips, or whatever else was available to create a delicious stew in the pressure cooker. She saw to it that there was enough to satisfy however many of us there were on hand. We ate a little better that fall and winter than we would have if the calf hadn't had his last meal in a patch of Johnson grass.

That entire episode made an indelible impression on me. It added greatly to my awareness that my Mother was one of the most remarkable and amazingly resourceful women in the world!

NANNY AND HER KIDS

Mother was convinced that goat's milk was easier to digest than cow's milk and particularly beneficial for small children. There were also times while our cows were pregnant that there wasn't enough milk to supply our needs. Goats were easier to feed and care for than cattle. They could even be tethered in our yard to mow the grass without danger to the younger brothers and sisters at play. These considerations led to the purchase of a petite light brown pregnant Toggenberg doe in 1933.

We children were delighted with this new addition to our extended household. We soon decided that her name was to be 'Nanny.' She was gentle and affectionate and loved to be petted. I think she even manifested a certain maternal affection for two-year-old Carl and Baby Martha. After all, she was in a sense to be their wet nurse.

Nanny's one-hundred-pound body expanded dramatically. About two months after she came to Bethany Homestead she showed signs of imminent motherhood. This event was to be my first on-the-scene obstetric experience. At age nine I had never before witnessed any animal giving birth. I found her lying in the shed threshing around in obvious distress. This upset me and I just wished that I knew how to help her. She actually did seem to appreciate that I was there petting and consoling her. There were intervening moments when she became more quiet and relaxed. After what seemed a long time a tiny head appeared and soon thereafter a struggling little body. I watched Nanny clearing the birth sac away from her kid and then rushed to the house to tell Mother, "Nanny has a baby!" For some reason none of my siblings were around. I rushed back out to the shed in time to see another little one appear. This called for a repeat trip to the house to report to Mother, "It's twins!" By the time I got back out a third little kid was emerging. My excitement mounted further as I rushed back to announce, "Now it's triplets!" I hurried back and spent some time watching Nanny clean up her babies and gently encourage them to have their first meals. Since she was only equipped to nourish two at a time this operation took some time. I made sure that the least aggressive little guy got his turn at the table. That night as I tried to go to sleep I counted baby goats popping out instead of sheep jumping over the fence.

Our trio of new babies consisted of a female and two males. We named them Fanny, Billy and Bob. We found them to be a delightful new set of playmates. They kept their mother's milk factory in high gear and grew rapidly. We didn't get much milk from Nanny until they were weaned. Thereafter she produced about two quarts daily. For my part, goat's milk didn't taste as good as that from our cows, but we dutifully drank it because it was supposed to be good for us.

A sad day arrived a few months later when Bob was sacrificed to add some protein calories to our diet. We felt like cannibals.

The passage of a year brought Billy and Fanny to physical maturity. He grew impressive horns, an aggressive spirit, and emanated the characteristic unpleasant odor of male goats. In time Fanny's girth increased and it became obvious that she was pregnant. When she delivered twin kids I started putting two and two together. There were no other male goats around so Billy had to be the father. How could he? Fanny was his sister! I was mortified by this scandalous development. I was even more shocked when Nanny became pregnant and also delivered twins! My childish affection for her was a little tainted by her incestuous relationship with her son. Paul and I had profound discussions about this matter. He commented that Billy was the father of his own little brother and sister. Nanny and her kids furnished me with a significant introduction to the critical facts of life and animal procreation.

Ingrid with Billy

LIVING OFF THE LAND

As we were growing up on Bethany Homestead a significant part of our food came from uncultivated natural sources. We learned from some of our traditional Ozarkian neighbors who were almost as much 'hunter-gatherers' as they were true farmers. Hunting and fishing provided a big part of their daily protein. The surrounding hills, forests and streams contained wild turkeys, rabbits, squirrels, possums, quail, fish, waterfowl, plus a few deer and wild hogs. All of these found their way onto the tables of the skilled hunters and fishermen of Southwest Missouri. Then there were all the goodies free for the taking from trees, bushes, and vines.

Our supply of meat from the great outdoors was limited by the complete absence of firearms in our home. Even during his days in the wilds of Africa Daddy didn't own a gun and certainly didn't see the need for one in our American home. That doesn't mean that we didn't exploit a lot of other possibilities for food from nature.

In the spring before the garden produced, Mother was out looking for fresh green shoots of wild spinach. When cooked correctly it tasted better than the domestic variety.

For some reason our orchard contained a plentiful supply of wild asparagus. This had probably originated in someone's garden and the seeds in the bright red berries brought to our property by birds. At any rate this gourmet vegetable was plentiful in early spring and added variety to our diet.

Another springtime treat came in the form of morel mushrooms which we found under fruit trees and in the woods after the rains. The typical sponge-on-a-stalk appearance could not be mistaken for any of the poisonous species. For safety's sake Mother refused to let us bring home any other kind. We kids felt that searching for these delicious treats was every bit as exciting as an Easter egg hunt and they were especially scrumptious fried in either bacon grease or butter.

By May berries were continuously available in different cycles until frost. First came wild strawberries from which Mother created the most delicious jam. I was addicted to their delectable flavor, and on at least three different occasions remember getting sick from eating too many while I was out picking. I didn't have that problem when I harvested intensely sour green gooseberries but our brother Paul loved their tartness. We all appreciated the preserves and pie which Mother made from them.

By mid-summer wild blackberries ripened and became Mother's fruit bonanza. As many of us children as were available and big enough would be furnished containers and sent out into the jungle of thorny vines. I remember Eunice as being the most diligent blackberry gatherer in our family. Mother would fire up her pressure cooker and convert the berries into jars of tasty blackberry sauce. She would feel that she hadn't adequately prepared for winter unless she had at least one hundred quarts. There was a dark side to the blackberry harvest. In addition to the hazard of the thorns, the vines were usually heavily infested with chiggers. The bites of these nasty little red mites was far worse than those inflicted by mosquitoes, and the itching continued for days. We never could figure out an effective prevention although we tried everything from kerosene to sulfur paste. The memory of that awful itching made the berries taste even better as we enjoyed them in the winter.

Sometime before frost we collected wild plums and grapes both of which made fine jelly. After the first frost had taken away the puckery taste we enjoyed eating persimmons. We liked to sample wild ground cherries which were also called Chinese lantern berries. Paul and I discovered that one of the hawthorn species produced a tasty little berry which was mostly seed but had a wonderful date-like flavor when chewed by the mouthful. Our neighbors called them 'black-haws.' We didn't have to go to the candy store to get our goodies.

In the fall there were nuts to collect and enjoy. We had a grove of about forty stately black walnut trees. When we harvested them and removed the green hulls our fingers were invariably stained brown for weeks. Cracking the nuts and removing the kernels was a tedious job, but the delicious flavor made the time well spent. Unfortunately most of the walnut trees died during one of the worst drought years. We had several species of hickory nuts. The only one worth processing was the so-called 'shag-barked hickory' which tasted much like a pecan. We found a few wild hazel nuts, also called filberts, along the fence rows.

I remember well when I first became aware of the novelty and excitement of fishing. Mother had fished with her family in the canal near their farm as a girl. When I was about six years old she persuaded Daddy to transport us to Pierson Creek about a mile from Bethany Homestead. There she introduced us to the art of dangling a worm on a hook in the stream. With her help we caught several little catfish and bluegills. She cleaned them herself and fried them in cornmeal batter. I'm not really a fish-fancier but they did taste good. That was the only fishing trip I remember taking as a family. When I was about twelve years old I persuaded my parents that I was old enough to fish on my own. I bought some hooks and sinkers, rigged a line on a limber sapling, dug a can of worms, and headed for the creek on a Sunday afternoon. I already knew where I was going to fish and settled down on the roots of a large tree overhanging the water. I was totally enthralled when my bobber cork danced briefly and then disappeared. I'll never forget the appearance of that first little bluegill (or sunfish as we called them). No other fish has given me a bigger thrill. I caught several others and some small bullhead catfish. Then I was surprised to pull out a small rainbow trout. We had heard that there were some in this spring-fed stream. Without a doubt it was the most beautiful fish in the world! I cleaned my catch as best as I knew and brought them home. Mother cooked them for lunch the next day. Over the next few years I spent many contented Sunday afternoons on the creek and thereby added a few protein calories to our diet.

Bethany Homestead contained a healthy population of cottontail rabbits. Our friendly neighbor David Creighton showed Paul and me how to construct box traps from boards or hollow logs. A door suspended over the front end is released by a trigger stick back inside the trap. Carrots or other fresh vegetables are used for bait. During the worst depression years we had many meals of fried or stewed rabbit. When times improved Paul and I shared the privilege of selling our bunnies to a produce house for ten to fifteen cents apiece for much-needed cash.

We captured other creatures besides rabbits. One morning I was excited to find one of the trapdoors down. On opening it I was astounded to find a baby bob white quail weighing less than an ounce. I still don't understand how he tripped the trap. I released him in a brushy corner hoping that his mother would find him.

Another day a horrific telltale odor told me a trap contained a skunk. I pulled up the door and judiciously got out of the way until that smelly creature disappeared into the underbrush. I never caught another rabbit in that trap.

In 1940 we caught very few rabbits and soon discovered that an epidemic of tularemia (rabbit fever) had nearly wiped out the cottontail population. Then of course we stopped trapping. We were fortunate that we weren't infected at that time. Two years later Mother nearly died from tularemia which she acquired through the bite of a tick.

In my early teen years a friend introduced me to another source of good food, bullfrogs: With a bright-beamed flashlight shining in their eyes it is possible to wade right up to them and pick them up. I made a number of successful forays along Pierson Creek and James River after I learned this technique. The flesh of frog legs is similar to the white meat of chickens and quite tasty.

All of these little gifts from nature made our diet a little more healthful and palatable over the years. And there was a certain degree of satisfaction and excitement in our various endeavors as amateur hunter-gatherers.

Veda, Ingrid and Eunice admiring apricot blossoms.

APPLES! APPLES! APPLES!

Our parents were excited that Bethany Homestead contained a large orchard. When they bought the place in 1930 they anticipated that the production and sale of fruit would supply a significant percentage of our family income. Unfortunately it didn't work out that way because of such factors as the depression, a devastating fire and the drought years.

Professor Chalfant, the previous owner, had been head of the music department at Drury College in Springfield. The fine pipe organ in the chapel there was named after him. Our neighbors, none of whom knew him well, weren't sure whether he was a bachelor or a widower. He didn't own a car so he drove the six miles from Springfield to the Homestead in a buggy or a one-horse wagon. He was usually accompanied by a Negro servant. Unfortunately Dr. Chalfant was a rank amateur as a horticulturist. He planted over one thousand apple trees of at least one hundred different species. Many of them were not compatible with Ozark climate and soil conditions. Others weren't suitable for marketing. Originally the soil hadn't been prepared properly and the trees hadn't been pruned, sprayed, or fertilized adequately.

The orchard also contained a few peach, pear, plum, and apricot trees. We children eagerly looked forward to the ripening of the Elberta peaches. Mother canned as many of them as possible. Only on one year of my decade in Springfield did we have any apricots because they always bloomed too early and the fruit was destroyed by frost.

Our Dad had learned to work hard while growing up on a Nebraska farm. I have vivid memories of how diligently he labored at pruning, clearing undergrowth, picking apples and all of the other endless tasks involved in fruit farming. In spring, spraying for fungus and insects was of critical importance. Our worst enemy was a creature known as the coddling moth, which laid its eggs on the apple. One or two larvae would burrow through and ruin the apple. The spray was composed of water containing arsenate of lead, sulfur and lime. It was mixed in a fifty-gallon wooden barrel mounted on a one-horse cart built much like an ancient Roman chariot and drawn by our old sway-back horse named Dolly. There was room on the platform by the barrel for a driver. One day a teen-age neighbor, Pete Rhoads, was giving us a hand. As he was driving the rig with old Dolly plodding slowly along he suddenly piped up singing the old Negro spiritual, "Good News! Chariot's Comin'! Good News! Chariot's Comin'!" Somehow this comical interlude reminded me of a scene out of the adventures of Don Quixote.

The pressure for the spray was generated by a large hand pump in the barrel wielded by the person driving the cart. Before Paul and I were strong enough to help, Mother was often the one to provide the muscle for that pump. I wish we had a video of our parents in action, Mother driving Old Dolly and pumping vigorously while Daddy wielded the eight-foot spray nozzle up into the highest branches of the trees. They were quite a team!

As they ripened we sampled all of the different varieties of apples to determine our favorites. The ones I preferred were Jonathans, Winesaps, and Stark's Delicious. We had several trees of a species called Twenty-ounce apples, so named because of the huge fruit produced. We weighed some which ranged up to sixteen-ounces but never found one literally living up to its twenty-ounce name. Mother favored a variety named Yellow Transparent, because when cooked the flesh disintegrated into a wonderfully flavored apple-sauce without pureeing. When ripe the peelings had a pale yellow color and indeed were almost transparent. They were also the earliest apples to ripen. Mother didn't feel that she had done her duty unless she canned at least a hundred quarts of Yellow Transparent applesauce. She also sun-dried many of the apples with good flavors.

When we children were old enough to wield a sharp knife we had the privilege of helping peel apples. Before long that chore got old and we were delighted when Daddy brought home a mechanical apple-peeler. You just impaled an apple on it and turned a crank. By rotating it carefully you could produce a nice peeling up to two-feet long.

One of the drawbacks of fruit trees was that they became attractive habitat for yellow jackets and wasps. Big black wasps an inch long built their large sunflower-shaped nests in apple trees. They were quite aggressive if you invaded their territory. Unlike honey bees, each could sting more than once. I remember becoming quite ill with fever, headache and nausea right after being stung four times when I accidentally bumped a wasp nest. Yellow jackets were even more of a nuisance because there were more of them. They built their nests underground near their source of food and they just loved ripe apples. We often went barefoot in the summer months and had to be careful when walking through the orchard. My ultimate close encounter came one day when I was eating a juicy ripe apple and talking to Paul. As I opened my mouth again I didn't notice that a yellow jacket had settled on the site of my previous bite and took him right into my mouth. He (or she) let me have it right on my tongue! And wow! That hurt! Supper didn't taste very good that evening. Since then I've been a bit more careful to examine what I put into my mouth.

On July 9, 1934, Daddy's forty-sixth birthday, we had gone without rain for weeks. A scorching sun beat down on Bethany Homestead. Knee-high sage grass had grown up throughout the orchard, then withered and dried in the heat. A brisk hot wind was blowing steadily from the southwest. Twelve-year-old brother Paul was in the orchard using match-heads as percussion caps in a toy pistol. Somehow the grass ignited and quickly the flames spread beyond control. We desperately tried to beat out the fire with wet burlap bags. Neighbors quickly came to the rescue, but before control was established one hundred of the best apple trees had been destroyed. Daddy was devastated, almost in tears. Poor Paul was equally stricken. His only punishment was observing the anguish our Dad was going through, but that was more than enough. Many other apple trees died that summer as a result of the severe heat and drought. So the summer of '34 was a tough one at our house.

We derived a definite satisfaction and pleasure in harvesting the apples once they ripened. In 1935 I kept a meticulous record of our daily activities. On June 14th we had our first fresh applesauce for supper. Between June 22nd and August 21st Paul, thirteen, and I, eleven years old, picked apples thirty-three full days and ten half-days. During the week of July 1-8 we picked a total of 118 bushels. This included both apples picked off the trees and windfalls gathered from the ground. Our greatest total was 35 bushels on July 3rd. For picking fruit out of reach from the ground we had an A-shaped ladder, the narrow top of which rested in the forks of higher branches. We had half-bushel fruit-picking canvas bags which buckled snugly around the shoulders and waist. When this container was full the fruit could be gently released by unsnapping the bottom and letting the apples roll into a basket.

How did we dispose of all this fruit? We sold what we could. The going price was between 15 and 25 cents per bushel. Even at those prices there weren't many takers. On July 4th that year we set up a little stand along the busy road which led down to a recreation area on the James River a mile away. We waited patiently from soon after dawn until nearly sunset and didn't sell a single apple. Every time a car went by we disappeared in cloud of dust. While waiting for customers Paul and I discovered that an apple made a wonderful hand grenade if you drilled a hole and inserted a firecracker. You then lit it, threw it high in the air and enjoyed a satisfying juicy explosion. I thought of exploding some of our bombs in front of oncoming cars to slow them down. Big brother Paul wisely vetoed that brainstorm.

At one time Daddy exchanged both apples and eggs for dental services with Dr. Kielbaugh. We also saw that our friends were well supplied with apples. Many of our overripe or windfall apples were fed to our pigs. In the dry times when grass was scarce, apples sometimes helped fill a void in the diet of our cattle and horses.

Most of our apples were converted into vinegar. During our second summer at Springfield Daddy bought a cider mill and a supply of small wooden kegs with a capacity of about fifteen gallons each. Apples were fed into a hopper over a crushing roller which was powered by a large hand crank. A heavy flywheel on the side opposite the crank helped maintain the necessary momentum to pulverize the fruit. At first Paul and I weren't strong enough to operate the crusher. We considered it something of a rite of passage to grow large enough and powerful enough to turn that handle and make the apples disappear into the jaws of that big machine. The pulp fell from the crusher into open-ended four-gallon cylinders made of closely spaced vertical wooden slats held together by two heavy steel hoops on the outside.

When the cylinder was full of crushed apples it was moved under the powerful press. A heavy wooden piston was fitted in the cylinder over the apple pulp and pressed down by turning the vertical worm-screw press. This forced the apple juice out between the slats of the cylinder. It then ran down into a container beneath the press. Additional force was applied with a four-foot wooden lever inserted between the handles of the wheel atop the worm screw. We were able to squeeze one to two gallons of juice out of a bushel of apples.

Fresh juice from nice ripe apples was delicious. We sometimes used it as a drink with meals, but most of it went into the wooden barrels where the action of microorganisms converted it into vinegar over a period of weeks. Microbial action caused the formation of a slimy rubbery membrane on the surface of the fermenting juice. For some reason this was called 'mother of vinegar.' When a thick layer had been formed, the vinegar seemed to be ready for use. It was then siphoned off into one-gallon glass jugs and sold for from fifteen to twenty-five cents per unit.

In the first few days after extraction the action of yeast produces a significant amount of ethyl alcohol in the juice and it becomes hard cider. Even as we got older I can't remember that either Paul or I ever experimented with its intoxicating properties.

On the very first days of operation of the cider mill Daddy filled five little barrels with apple juice. Assuming that they should be sealed he pounded the wooden corks tightly into the bungholes on the side of the kegs and stored them in a shed attached to the barn.

Three nights later Paul and I were sleeping out under the stars about fifty yards away. Suddenly we were awakened by a mighty explosion, "Ka-Pow!" A few moments later an identical double explosion shattered the stillness of the night. Daddy rushed out to investigate and discovered that two of his kegs had blown their corks. The first report came as the cork blew out and the second as it hit the ceiling. There was no spillage of the fermenting cider. Daddy gingerly pried the corks loose on the other three kegs creating three more explosions. He was careful to stay out of the way of the flying projectiles.

In my teen years I found another use for the cider press. A significant rural industry in the Ozarks was making sorghum. The juice was pressed out of sorghum cane, distantly related to sugar cane, by a rotary press. This was powered by a mule walking in circles as the cane was drawn into the device like clothes into a washing machine wringer. The juice was collected and boiled for hours over a slow fire as is done in the production of maple syrup. The end product is honey-colored sorghum, often used as a sugar-substitute in the Ozarks. We thought it was especially tasty on pancakes.

I decided to attempt sorghum manufacturing on my own. We had some millet cane planted for cattle forage which was very similar to that used to produce sorghum. I chopped up the stalks into small pieces with a machete and squeezed out the juice with the cider press. I scrubbed out a ten-gallon container which had been used to water our cattle. It had been made by cutting a hot water tank in half lengthwise. I mounted it on rocks about six inches off the ground. Under this I built a wood fire and simmered my cane-juice intermittently for two days. I ended up with about two quarts of thick dark syrup which I spooned out of the tank into pint jars and presented to Mother. She congratulated me on my effort but not on the quality of my product. The sweetness was present but adulterated by a smoky bitter metallic flavor, nothing like the delicious sorghum created by our neighbors. I was the only one brave enough to try it on Mother's pancakes. I managed to get them down but had to acknowledge that it wasn't fit for human consumption. My only consolation was that our dog Pal thought it tasted great. That ended my foray into the sorghum business.

Bethany Homestead has now largely been engulfed by a subdivision of the city of Springfield. The only surviving apple tree of Professor Chalfant's thousand-tree orchard shades part of my sister Veda's backyard. When we visit her I love to go out, lay my arms on that gnarled and sturdy trunk, shut my eyes, and let the memories flow.

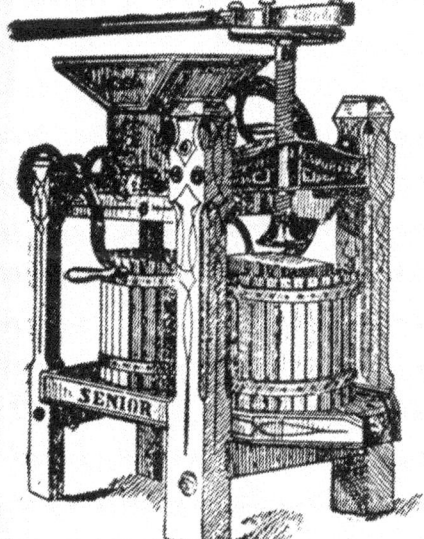

A cider mill similar to the one we used, as listed in a vintage Sears catalog.

THE OLD SWIMMING HOLE

The recreational activity which meant the most to us boys in the hot Ozark summertime was swimming. We could only enjoy a refreshing dip after we had completed all of our chores. This provided a special incentive to be as diligent and swift as possible in fulfilling our daily responsibilities.

Paul and I learned to swim in our muddy pond. Our sisters didn't participate so there was no need for bathing suits. The favored stroke was the 'dog-paddle' which I think we learned from watching our dogs Von and Pal. Both of them enjoyed the water as much we did. I was proud when I could swim the forty feet across the pond without stopping. At one end the water was six feet deep in the springtime so we rigged up a plank for a diving board. After a long winter we eagerly looked forward to balmier weather and usually had our first swim in late February or early March. Depending upon the rainfall the water level dropped during the warm weather and the surface was colonized by a layer of scummy, stringy green algae. That didn't keep us out of the pond after a hot day until we were a little older.

As we approached adolescence swimming in the pond became less appealing. We started escaping to two different sites on the James River a mile away. This stream was spring-fed and the water quite clear most of the time. Our favorite hole had a cable swing attached to a branch thirty feet up in a huge sycamore tree. We could fly far out over the water and jump or dive into a deep hole. This site was right on the river road so we did have to wear bathing suits. I have many happy memories of evenings spent with friends at that special place. Every time we visit the Ozarks I like to drive by the old swimming hole to refresh those recollections.

Other swimmers in both the pond and the river made us a bit anxious. One day Paul and I saw a huge snapping turtle crawl into our pond. His shell was at least a foot in diameter and he had a big ugly head. One of our adult neighbors assured us that we didn't have to worry about swimming with that monster because he was at least as afraid of us as we were of him. The river offered an even more fearsome inhabitant. One day we had just arrived at our favorite hole on the James. Before we had entered the water a canoe occupied by a young couple came gliding silently upstream in front of us. As they passed us we were startled to see a large black snake streak from the bank toward the canoe. It apparently mistook the paddle for a fish, and latched onto it. The young woman screamed as she lifted her paddle out of the water with a writhing four-foot snake attached. As soon as he recognized his mistake he let go and retreated as fast as he had attacked. The poor girl screamed hysterically and we weren't so sure we wanted to go swimming with that creature around. One of our older friends identified the snake as a cottonmouth or water moccasin. He reassured us that the serpent wouldn't attack a human swimming and blithely dove into the river to prove it. I still was a little hesitant, but finally joined the rest of my friends in the water.

When I was eleven years old a near-drowning experience took away some of the joy of swimming for a few months. Our 4-H club scheduled a swimming party picnic at a little park on the James River. Paul couldn't attend so I walked the mile from our house to the picnic site and arrived before anybody else from our group. Other swimmers whom I didn't know were on hand. I decided to get a head start on my friends, put on my bathing suit and hurried into the water. My first goal was to swim across the river and back, a distance which I had easily accomplished many times in our pond. The first crossing went smoothly but on the way back I ran out of gas. I hadn't made allowances for the force of the current which carried me into deeper water. At the point of exhaustion I thought I was close enough to the bank to let my feet down and wade the rest of the way. That was a mistake! My feet didn't find the bottom and I panicked. The current was carrying me into deeper water and I forgot all of what little that I knew about swimming. The swift water carried me under as I struggled desperately and fruitlessly.

When I surfaced the first time I saw several adult swimmers only a few feet away and I yelled for assistance, "Help! I'm drowning!" As I went under again my whole life seemed to flash by in front of me. I especially remember a vision of my parents, brothers, sisters, and friends standing around my coffin weeping. When I surfaced again and saw that none of the nearby swimmers was coming to my assistance I remember a feeling of intense anger. I screamed at them to please come and help me to no avail. I was just about ready to give up when the current carried me against a partially submerged log projecting out into the river from the other side. I grasped it desperately and, coughing and sputtering, dragged myself up on the opposite bank. It wasn't necessary to swim back because there was a wide shallow wadeable stretch of water fifty yards upstream.

I didn't go back in the water that day. When the rest of our group arrived I didn't tell them about my horrible experience. They wondered why I didn't go swimming with them and I made the excuse that I just wasn't feeling well. Nor did I share the story of my narrow escape with my family for several months. And I didn't write a word about it in my diary. Swimming was not really enjoyable for me again for about another year. When I did go back into the water I made up my mind to become a good enough and wise enough swimmer not to let something like that happen again.

With the approach of adolescence there came a new dimension to the appeal of public swimming, namely, girls in bathing suits. That was one of the reasons for which at the age of fourteen I thoroughly enjoyed attending a summer 4-H club camp. A reporter for the Springfield newspaper snapped a photo of me showing off to a pair of fair lassies. Neither of them seemed to be the least bit impressed.

In the summer of 1941 I attended a week-long camp for the FFA, (Future Farmers of America). About one hundred high school boys attended. We went swimming twice daily in a lovely lake with clear water and a sandy bottom.

I was proud of being able to swim farther underwater than most of my friends. For years, Mr. Barrow, my vocational agriculture teacher, liked to remind me of an incident at that FFA camp. We were having a contest to see who could go the farthest underwater without a breath. I determined that if I could swim behind a floating dock about thirty yards from the diving platform I could put on a major disappearing act. This I did, swimming deep under the rope barrier and surfacing behind the dock so nobody could see me. I remained concealed just long enough to really scare my friends. I heard Mr. Barrow anxiously calling out, "What happened to John? He must be in trouble!" After pulling myself up on the floating dock I called, "Here I am!" The teachers were pretty upset with me and forbade any more underwater shenanigans. Fifty-seven years later I had breakfast with Mr. Barrow and he said that he still hadn't forgiven me for that trick!

To this day I enjoy going for a dip and swimming a mile almost daily in Corvallis pools. There's no better exercise at any age.

"TAKE ME OUT TO THE BALL GAME!"

Softball was far and away the most popular recreational activity for us boys, and for some of the girls, at Blackman School. Following the St. Louis Cardinals and the Browns on the radio and in the newspapers was bigtime for Paul and me. Baseball and boxing were the only professional sports of which we were aware. When the daily paper arrived we turned first to the sports page to see what our heroes had done the day before. Of course every red-blooded boy had his private dreams of becoming a major league star.

The only equipment we had at school was a beat-up old bat and a mangy softball. One year we broke the bat and Paul laboriously carved out a monstrous club from a small hickory tree. It was so heavy that we little kids could barely swing it but it had to do until we scraped together enough cash to buy a new 'Louisville Slugger.' A couple of the guys had their own personal gloves which they would sometimes reluctantly share.

The most common game format involved the two best players choosing up sides. An important part of this ritual was determining who got to choose first. One captain threw the bat to the other which he caught with one hand. The other grasped it just above this and they alternately marched their hands up to the tip of the handle. The one who obtained the final hold at the end chose first. This was important because there was quite a variation in the baseball skills of the 'candidates' for the teams.

I was never one of the first ones chosen. My foot-speed, reflexes, and coordination all had their limitations. But I never gave up and in time there was a little improvement. I was strong enough so that if I did happen to hit the ball solidly it went a good distance.

We whiled away many happy recesses and noon hours playing ball. It was always difficult to break up the game and go back to the books when the bell rang. One year we had enough players to make up a team of ten. We challenged one of the neighboring, much larger schools to a game. Oak Grove had nearly a hundred students and three teachers. Both schools recognized that such a game would be a mismatch. They proposed that the Blackman team play the Oak Grove fourth, fifth, and sixth-graders. They had a skinny little pitcher who didn't appear at all imposing until he started mowing us down with his fastball. According to my diary they beat us 18-0. I lucked out and got one of the three hits he gave up. That was something of a personal moral victory. That was the only interscholastic competition we ever had but we still had lots of intramural fun at our home park.

The stories Mother told us about her brother Bill played a big part in making baseball come alive for Paul and me. We especially liked the one about how he had acquired his nickname 'Baby Doll.' On the opening day of the 1912 Southern League season in Mobile, Alabama, the sun was shining and the stands were full. The band played and the crowd sang a popular tune of that day, "Oh, You Beautiful Doll!" As they finished, a lanky, gangly 21-year-old rookie named Bill Jacobson stepped into the batter's box and hit the first pitch over the center field fence for a prodigious home run. A portly Negro lady in the colored section with a powerful voice, yelled out so all could hear, "That's that Baby Doll we was just singin' about!" At that moment a crowd favorite and a nickname were born. Bill was called Baby Doll for the rest of his life.

He went on to become a star outfielder with the St. Louis Browns with a lifetime batting average of .311. He batted over .300 for seven consecutive seasons, with a peak of .355 in 1920. That year he also led the American League in runs batted in, until near the end when Babe Ruth surpassed him by just three. In 1921 the New York Yankees beat out the Browns by just a half game to thwart Baby Doll's dream of playing in the World Series. He was proudest of the fact that at one time he held 13 different major league fielding records, the last of which was broken by Joe DiMaggio 24 years later. In the 1950's he was voted the all-time best centerfielder of the Browns. He himself said that he loved to watch Willie Mays because he reminded him of his own style of fielding. Bill Jacobson's best contract earned him $15,000 over two years. He took that bonanza and bought a fine 80-acre farm in Illinois where he worked diligently for the rest of his productive years.

When I went to medical school in St. Louis in the late 40's I liked to try out different barbershops. The subject of discussion was frequently baseball and I would casually ask, "Have you ever heard of Baby Doll Jacobson?" The inevitable response was that he was one of the great ones. Then of course I would proudly say, "He's my uncle!"

Back in the Ozarks we had also become St. Louis Cardinal fans. Springfield had a farm team which was often the last stopping place of players on the way up to the majors. Joe Garagiola, as a 15-year-old high school student, already had some sort of tentative agreement with the Cardinals. When school was out in the spring he came to Springfield to work out with our class AA farm team. I remember seeing his picture in the paper wearing his catcher's paraphernalia and sporting a goatee. He was just my age and I don't know which I envied more, his baseball prowess or his ability to grow a beard.

We eagerly followed our local Cardinals in the paper and sometimes on the radio. Paul had rigged up a crystal set radio which picked up the Springfield station. It was made from a chunk of lead crystal we had picked up in a nearby lead mine, a coil, and a telephone receiver. At night in our boys' cottage or sleeping out under the stars, we could follow the course of the game when everybody else in our family was asleep. That was special!

Personally attending a professional baseball game was an unattainable luxury until I was 15 years old. Paul and I then had jobs getting up at 3:30 AM and milking a neighbor's thirty cows by hand. This provided us with some spending money. The Springfield Cardinals had a week-night double-header with the Joplin team. The main attraction was a phenomenal 17-year-old player named Stan Musial who was batting over .400 and being touted as a potential superstar. Daddy had evening business in town but couldn't stay for the game. We assured him that we were certain to get a ride home with a neighbor. Daddy delivered us to White City Baseball Park, eight miles from our house. We bought the cheapest bleacher seat tickets and joined the excited crowd. Lively organ music made the occasion even more festive. The Cardinals won both games thanks largely to Stan Musial's hitting. He pounded out a home run, a triple, a double and two singles, plus fielding flawlessly. We kept looking around for our neighbor but somehow missed him. By the end of the second game it was nearly 1:00 AM and we had no alternative but to walk the eight miles home. We were exhausted when we dragged in at 3:00 AM, just in time to walk to Fallon's dairy and milk his thirty cows again. I think part of the time I was milking in my sleep. But Paul and I agreed that if we had it to do over again we wouldn't hesitate to repeat our long walk home.

Uncle Bill's baseball card, distributed free with a candy bar. I bought it for $15.00 in 1997.

I have now been a Cardinal fan for 70 years. Those early years were exciting, following such heroes as Dizzy Dean, Ducky Medwick, Whitey Kurowski, Red Schoendienst, and, of course, 'Stan the Man' Musial. In 1944 the army sent me to school in St. Louis and I lived there for a total of six years. That indelibly stamped my attachment to the Redbirds. The Browns remained my American League favorites although they didn't do much after their triumphant march to the World Series in 1944. The Cardinals also won the National League pennant that year and I was in the stands at Sportsman Park to watch two games of the All-St. Louis world series. I had mixed feelings about whom I favored. The Cardinals prevailed four games to two but Baby Doll's Browns played well.

The Brown's declining attendance in the following years prompted futile efforts to save the franchise. They pulled such stunts as hiring a midget as a leadoff batter, and signing a one-armed outfielder named Pete Gray. He was actually a bonafide major leaguer and I marveled at his fielding ability. I got to see him hit a one-armed home run. The Browns moved to Washington D.C. where they became the Senators. Later on, the franchise was moved to Minneapolis and they became the Minnesota Twins. Up until now the Twins have been my sentimental American League favorites because they're literally the grandchildren of my beloved Browns. My modern Cardinals tend to collapse at inappropriate times, but they are still my favorite.

LEARNING BY DOING IN THE 4-H CLUB

My diary entry for June 28, 1935, reads, "We joined a 4-H calf club today and found it quite interesting." About a dozen of us, ages 10-17, met at a neighbor's home. Involvement with this organization over the next four years added much fun, excitement and some practical lessons to an otherwise humdrum life on the farm. The national 4-H club organization grew out of local programs to broaden the horizons of rural and small-town youth. In 1914 the US Dept. of Agriculture was commissioned by Congress to facilitate and fund the organizations which eventually became the 4-H Club. By 1924 every state and US territory was involved. A choice of over fifty different projects was available, from training sled dogs in Alaska to raising cotton in the South. The 4-H club motto is "Make The Best Better!"

Each member of our local club was expected to help raise a calf or conduct another dairy-related project. Meticulous records were expected plus evidence of hands-on involvement. Several members had registered purebred Jersey or Guernsey calves which they planned to show at fairs and livestock competitions. Our plebeian crossbreed calves at home were definitely not qualified for exhibition but Paul and I were not treated as second-class citizens.

At the initial meeting we began by learning the 4-H pledge:
"I pledge
My head to clearer thinking,
My heart to greater loyalty,

My hands to larger service,
My health to better living,
    for my club, my community, and my country."

(As I was preparing to write this I called a Corvallis family active in 4-H work to see if I had the pledge right after not having repeated it for over sixty years. I was pleased to learn that my memory hadn't failed me. The only difference is that the words, 'my world' have been added to the ending.)

Our meetings were about fifty percent business and study, and the rest of the time was devoted to fun, games, and singing. At that first meeting one of the members had brought his older cousin, a well-known young professional wrestler. We were awed by this specimen whose massive muscles bulged visibly through his shirt. He wore a bow tie and had acquired the skill of making it bounce up and down by oscillating his Adam's apple. I had never seen that trick before and resolved to add it to my repertoire. When Mother saw me practicing in front of a mirror she scolded me with the warning that my Adam's apple would stick out like a turkey's if I continued those antics. She was too late; my exhibitionist genes were already programmed. That little trick has been an integral part of my career as a pediatrician and as a grandfather.

The 4-H Club program is promoted and guided by state and county agricultural extension agents. Our county agent was Mr. C.C. Keller, a handsome charismatic gentleman who became one of my heroes and role models. He was present at our first organizational meeting and really generated enthusiasm. He had been a star athlete in college. He had grown up on a farm in Arkansas and we were told that he could pick up a 500-pound bale of cotton and carry it on his back. At one of our county 4-H Roundups we competed in a 100-yard dash. I was astounded that Mr. Keller started the race by firing a pistol, ran down ahead of all of us and was there at the finish line to greet the winners. After retirement he was to become a much loved and appreciated Baptist minister. He lived on into his nineties and was active to the end.

The backbone of local leadership was formed by volunteer adults. Maude Ingram, wife of a local dairy farmer and mother of one of our members, stands out in my memory as the one who made our club function effectively. She took us all under her wings but saw to it that we toed the line. Much of the time our meetings were held at her house. She always had a special treat at refreshment time, often homemade ice cream.

Practical demonstrations of specific work activities were emphasized in 4-H work. In 1938 a good friend, Glen Pursley, and I developed a demonstration, "The Production of Clean Milk." We went through a simple routine of cleaning utensils, washing the cow's udder, etc. We won first place in both county and state contests and were invited to enter the national competition at the Mid-South Fair in Memphis, Tennessee, the first week in September. The event was of a high enough priority to justify a week out of school. Mr. Keller drove us to Memphis, passing through the area in which he had grown up in Northern Arkansas. I was intrigued to see rice and cotton plantations for the first time. We didn't win any prizes with our demonstration but enjoyed all facets of the big fair. We stayed at a nice hotel. Neither Glen nor I had ever stayed in one before so we felt that we were living in luxury. One evening we were joined on the elevator by a strikingly-dressed young woman leading two poodles. She looked familiar. Later Mr. Keller informed us that we had shared our elevator with the one and only Sally Rand. She was nationally famous for her exotic dances in which she pirouetted around the stage with only large rubber bubbles or feather fans as costumes. Glen and I were disappointed that Mr. Keller didn't offer to take us to see her perform.

One summer Sidney Ingram, Glen and I represented our club as a dairy judging team. We were presented with classes of four cows of a specific breed which we were to rank in order of probable milk productivity, breed characteristics, etc. An important part of the competition was declaration of the reasons for the rank assigned each animal. We won both the Greene County and Missouri State 4-H judging contests and went to 'The Big One' at the National Dairy Show in Waterloo, Iowa. We were doing well. Our leader informed us that we were tied for the lead with another team after the first three classes. We just had the class of Jerseys left to evaluate. For some reason I always had difficulty ranking that breed. As it turned out I completely reversed the ranking established by the judges. I had picked the worst cow as best, and the best as worst. That toppled us from our pedestal. Sidney was really upset with me and never let me forget that dismal performance. With tongue in cheek I told him that all Jerseys looked alike to me so I decided to pick the one with the prettiest eyes. That was the end of my dairy judging career. By the way, Sid became a veterinarian and Glen went on to earn a doctorate in dairy husbandry.

Another objective of 4-H clubs is to promote communication and organization. Even with a small club we were required to conduct our meetings in the format dictated by Robert's Rules of Orders. In my second year I was elected as club reporter. This not only involved publicizing our activities but required giving reports at the club meetings. On May 2, 1936, I gave a detailed report on caring for a calf from birth until the age of six weeks.

Red-haired, 14-year-old John Hult, Springfield farm boy, is demonstrating his prowess as a swimmer—or a ducker—to an admiring feminine audience composed of Kathryn Salts, of Willard, and Rosalie Martin of Mount Vernon. There's a fine swimming hole in the James for the 4-H campers, and when all 130 of them are in, the water is literally alive with boys and girls. County Agent Keller has devised a plan to eliminate the danger when so many are swimming at once, and it is now being adopted by those in charge of camps all over the country. Each swimmer has a "swimming partner." At frequent intervals, Keller or whoever is in charge of the swimming hour blows a whistle, and when the whistle blows, everyone is supposed to reach out and touch his partner. If he's too far away for that, he returns immediately, and is thereby reminded that he's responsible for the safety of his teammate.

Published in the *Springfield Leader and Press*, July 19th, 1938.

The year 1937 coincided with my awakening to an intense interest in and attraction to members of the opposite sex. Each 4-H club meeting was like an oasis in the desert. I was small for my age with bad teeth, red hair and freckles. The girls certainly didn't beat a path to my doorstep. That didn't keep me from worshipping them from afar. I distinctively recall how exciting it was to attend the three-day 4-H camp on the James River in July, 1938. The proximity of pretty girls, other than my sisters, set my heart to doing flip-flops. We had good food and all sorts of fun, stimulating activities, but my dominant memory now is just the presence of lovely young ladies. My most poignant memory was that of the campfire sing-along on the last night at camp. I had the privilege of sitting next to one of the most attractive girls in camp in the circle around the fire as we sang "The Four-leaf Clover Song:"

"I know a place where the sun is like gold.
Where the cherry blooms burst like snow.
And down underneath is the loveliest nook,
Where the four-leaf clovers grow."

My 4-H club years taught me some good lessons and generated many happy memories.

MY SABBATICAL YEAR

May 10, 1937, was my last day of the eighth grade at Blackman School. We were given the results of the final examinations we had finished the previous week. According to my diary I averaged 92% on the thirteen different subjects upon which we were tested. A festive atmosphere prevailed and we celebrated the occasion with a picnic down on the James River. The teacher, Mrs. Strong, and several parents transported the student body of about twenty-four on a warm spring morning. I believe the luncheon menu included hot dogs and marshmallows. Going into the water was forbidden so we had to be content with land-based fun and games. The outing was a success but I experienced real sadness at leaving friends and departing forever from the school activities which had meant so much to me.

Five days later my parents took me, along with Warren McAllister, the only other Blackman eighth grader that year, to the county graduation exercises in Springfield. We were seated in a large auditorium with rows upon rows of proud parents and neatly dressed boys and girls. I enjoyed the special music and even the speech by the county superintendent. For an educator he had the appropriate name of Dr. Study. He complimented us on our achievement and urged us to continue our education into high school. Many of the group would not do so, including my classmate Warren. Rural parents often thought that eight grades of schooling was enough and they needed both the boys and the girls to help them on the farm and in the home.

For graduation gifts my family gave me books, a baseball glove, and a pair of tennis shoes. Uncle Lenus, Daddy's youngest brother, gave me my first watch, a shiny new Ingersoll. That unexpected thrill quickly ended in a broken heart. When it came in the mail I wound it and strapped it on my wrist. Paul and I were ready to go swimming and walked the mile down to the river. I eagerly undressed and dived off the bank into the water, forgetting to take off my new treasure. My mistake flashed through my mind as I surfaced and I hurried out of the stream. But Alas! The damage was done and the watch was unfixable by the time we got it to a jeweler. I was unable to afford another watch until I went into the army six years later. My thank you letter to Uncle Lenus said nothing about my great tragedy.

I was looking forward to going to Rogersville High School where Paul was completing his freshman year. Mr. George Riley, the principal, had sent me a letter inviting me to visit school the following week. When that big day came I rode the bus with Paul and had an exciting day visiting classes including music rehearsals, physical education activities and perhaps a little girl-watching. Those high school girls were decidedly more exciting than my Blackman School classmates of the tender gender. I was enthused about continuing my education at the next level.

At the same time I realized that my schooling might have to wait. Paul had voluntarily stayed out for a year after finishing Blackman School to help out at home. Daddy was the oldest of seven children and hadn't been able to go to high school until he was eighteen. Mother's brother, Verne Jacobson, stayed home to help Grandpa on the farm for a year before going to the ninth grade. So this practice was something of a tradition on both sides of our family and widespread in rural Midwest communities. Boys were needed on their home farms and could really prove that they were seriously intent on further education by staying home and working for a year or so.

My parents were still totally committed to seeing that their children had the opportunity to go to high school and then on to college. We had a family meeting and the consensus was that my staying home for a year would help considerably. Daddy was being urged to be available to serve as interim pastor in different Lutheran churches out of state. He would have been hesitant to do so if one of us older boys wasn't home to help Mother on the farm. I volunteered that it was my turn to be the full-time farmer although I would rather have been in school. Our parents were aware of that and really expressed their gratitude for my decision.

Since I had skipped from the second to the fourth grade I would have been a year younger than my ninth grade classmates. That made the decision easier. I was only twelve and a half years old. My diary indicates that I was only five feet tall and weighed 94 pounds. My 11½-year-old sister Ingrid was three inches taller and a little heavier. I was quite immature physically with a high-pitched soprano voice and was emotionally pre-adolescent. I was intensely eager to learn but career-wise had no idea what I wanted to do with my life. All things considered, that year at home was a good decision. You might say that I was being 'red-shirted' for the good of the team and to enhance my career potential.

Thus began my sabbatical year, the only one I ever had. Seven years sufficed to complete eight grades and now I was going to head into a different lifestyle. Hopefully there would be some peak experiences to balance out the valleys I suspected I would trudge through.

My year out of school officially began with the first day of the school year. On Monday, August 30th, 1937, I enviously watched Paul hurry away to catch the bus to Rogersville High School at 7:30 AM. Ingrid, Veda, Eunice and Carl excitedly trekked through the orchard to join their friends at Blackman School. Happy shouts and laughter carried to our house from the playground one hundred yards away, culminating with the ringing of the bell which called the children inside. My secret heart cried out, "I'm not certain I'm going to like this staying out of school for a whole year!" I gathered my equipment, went out into the orchard and began picking apples with a big lump in my throat. Mother must have sensed what I was going through and called me to the house for coffee and rusks at mid-morning. She knew me well and said things which made me feel better. Later that week my diary reads, "It sure is hard to get along without Paul."

Those first weeks with five of my siblings coming home excited about their school experiences were painful. Judging from the apathetic colorless entries in my diary, I must have been significantly depressed. The fact that I was small for my age bothered me. I was afraid to smile because my front teeth were badly decayed. I was also convinced that my red hair placed me in a undesirable minority group. I had never conquered my bedwetting problem and it seemed to be getting worse. A distinct attraction to the opposite sex was already budding within me but I suffered from the doubt that any girl would ever be interested in me. My family continued to let me know that they appreciated and cared for me. And I really enjoyed interacting with my three pre-school siblings, Martha, Gustav, and Mary. Still all of the above-listed negative factors tilted the scale in the wrong direction.

As time went by certain events transpired, I made some adjustments, and started feeling better about myself. I got a job milking regularly for Mr. Fallon, which provided both cash and a little pride of accomplishment. On September 29, the entire family made a memorable trip to Mother's parents' golden wedding anniversary celebration in Northern Illinois. I thoroughly enjoyed getting acquainted with the colorful Jacobson clan of aunts, uncles and cousins. That is a story in itself which will be told separately.

Another major happening which brought me a measure of self-esteem was Daddy's call to serve a church in Osceola, Nebraska. That gave me the responsibility of taking our produce to market and doing the family shopping. How was this to be accomplished when Daddy took our only car with him to Nebraska? Arrangements were made with a generous friendly neighbor, Spence Rhoads, who had a daily milk-collecting route past our house. His teen-aged son Pete picked up ten-gallon cans of milk and cream from several farms in his truck and delivered them to produce houses in Springfield. He would have room to take me and our cream and eggs to market twice weekly and haul home my purchases. The responsibility of the produce-marketing and family shopping to some extent made me the man of the house and boosted my ego considerably.

On a typical market day Pete would pick me up at 7:30 along with our five-gallon can of cream and a crate containing twelve to fifteen dozen eggs. Pete was a jolly young man who sang as he drove. Often he told clever stories. He enjoyed teasing me but never in a demeaning manner. He drove me to Swift and Company's collection station and left me there with my cream and eggs. I waited while these were being measured and tested. My diary indicates that our cream tested as high as 48% butterfat. At least some of the eggs were candled to determine their freshness.

In about an hour I collected in cash the money for our produce and walked several blocks to the Colonial Bakery's week-old bread department. I purchased from fifty to one hundred pounds of bakery goods which had been returned after exceeding the shelf life in the stores. The cost was one cent per pound. We fed this to our chickens, pigs, and even cows. The freshest loaves ended up on our kitchen table. Sometimes the bag from the bakery contained still-edible cakes and rolls which were eagerly rescued and enjoyed.

Then I walked to Safeways where I carefully filled Mother's grocery list. Sometimes I made a short side-trip to another local grocery store which often brought in railroad carloads of bananas from New Orleans. These sold for ten cents per dozen and were a special treat at our house. On one occasion I took one of my own precious dimes, picked out twelve nice ripe bananas and consumed them all before the homeward trip. I had heard that they were good to put on the weight I was anxious to add to my skinny frame.

If there was still time I walked to Woolworth's five-and-ten cent store on the city square. This was a wonderful place to run into friends and neighbors. I was already addicted to caffeine and the snack bar sold a cup of coffee with a free donut for a nickel. My final stop was the Missouri Farmer's Association feed store where Pete usually suggested meeting me. Here I purchased feed such as 'shorts,' a wheat flour milling by-product sold in one-hundred-pound bags. Another occasional purchase was twenty-five-gallon drums of 'semi-solid buttermilk,' a highly-concentrated dairy product fed to our livestock. My purchases were loaded into Rhoad's truck. There was still a detour to the bakery to pick up my load of bread before we returned home. I don't believe these generous neighbors accepted any money for all the hauling they did for us during the several months this shopping arrangement went on. They knew we were struggling financially. I distinctly remember my parents agonizing about even having enough money to pay the interest on the mortgage on Bethany Homestead.

Those shopping adventures became a welcome diversion for me during the time I was out of school, but there was much to do when I got back home.

In 1937 there were 1001 different jobs to be done on our orchard-farm. A few entries from my diary indicate some of our activities:

May 19: Paul and I sprayed 87 apple trees using 5 fifty-gallon barrels of spray.

May 20: I planted corn this morning.

June 5: I pulled weeds in the morning and cut wood in the afternoon. (From about 1937 on, Paul and I cut every stick of wood which fueled Mother's cook-stove and our pot-bellied heating stove in the living room. The amount we produced over the years with an ax, bucksaw, or cross-cut saw would have added up to an impressive mountain.)

June 8: I planted 13 hills of watermelons and several rows of popcorn.

June 11: I sprayed all the cabbage plants in the morning and planted tomatoes in the afternoon.

June 21: Today was my 13th birthday. I hauled in hay all morning and a good part of the afternoon. The rest of the time I just took off and went swimming.

June 26: I planted stuff all day. (I'm uncertain what kind of 'stuff' it was, probably tomatoes, pumpkins, or pole beans. The latter were planted next to the corn so the vines would have something on which to climb.)

July 7: I picked 7½ bushels of Early Harvest and one of Henry Clay apples.

July 19: I was laid up with a boil on my leg and couldn't work outside so I helped Mother. I shelled beans in the morning and peeled apples in the afternoon.

Aug. 19: I picked 28 bushels of Maidenblush and Wealthy apples.

Aug. 27: Paul and I made cider for vinegar all day.

Gus Fallon was a wealthy entrepreneur from Springfield who owned the farm west of us. He had amassed a fortune during WWI procuring mules for the US Army. There was space in his barns for several hundred mules. After the war that business collapsed and he turned to dairy farming, but he knew more about mules than he did about milk-producing cattle. He bought scrub cows at auction for the lowest possible prices. He sold his milk to a Mr. Gray who had set up his pasteurization and bottling operation on the farm. Mr. Fallon had a bad reputation as an employer, paying the lowest possible wages. Many of his employees had been recruited on

Springfield's 'skid row' district and there were frequent turnovers. That's where the Hult boys came in. Mr. Fallon had discovered that we were good milkers and he often called and said, "I don't have anybody to milk my cows tonight! Could you give me a hand?" We always said yes.

There was no such thing as a milking machine. He paid us less than ten cents an hour and we milked up to thirty cows. On one occasion when Paul had to stay overnight at the high school, I milked all thirty cows by myself. Six years later little brother Carl, only 10 years old, milked 30 of Mr. Fallon's cows by himself when I didn't get home from high school in time. That sounds a little abusive, according to child labor laws, but Carl thought it was great fun. These low-grade cattle only gave about a gallon of milk twice daily but it added up to 30 gallons per milking. In the morning we had to finish milking by 6:30 so Mr. Gray could process and bottle it. Then we went home and milked our own cows.

Another employer who called on me frequently in the spring and summer was our neighbor, Mrs. Larimer. My job at her house was keeping her garden as weed-free as possible. She was proud of her lovely gladiolas and I had to be careful not to injure them as I hoed. Her standard wage was five cents per hour and it was never increased. On hot days she would occasionally bring out a pitcher of lemonade for a refreshing break. One day I had worked five hours and she paid me off with a shiny new quarter. I was walking the quarter of a mile home when a friend drove by with his team of horses pulling a wagon loaded with loose hay. His offer for a ride was accepted and I crawled up into the soft fragrant alfalfa. I began flipping my quarter into the air and catching it. The wagon hit a bump and lurched as the coin was in the air and it dropped deep into the hay. I desperately scrambled after it but the fruit of my five hours of labor had disappeared forever. That was an awful moment in my young life. I woefully reported my tremendous loss to Mother but not to Mrs. Larimer. She would have been sympathetic but probably wouldn't have felt a responsibility to give me any disaster relief.

One day in the spring of 1938 Mrs. Larimer called me for a special project. She was having some male chicks caponized, or if you will, castrated, by a young pre-medical student acquaintance named Dallas Anthony. He needed somebody to be his surgical assistant. At that time I had no idea that I would some day be a physician, but was much intrigued by the procedure. As I held the chick, Doctor-to-be Dallas made an incision behind the last rib with a wicked looking scalpel. He gave me a retractor to keep the wound open while he reached in and skillfully excised the internal testicle. My stomach did flip-flops and I got a little dizzy, but I managed to remain upright. The surgery was then repeated on the opposite side. None of our patients died, and all grew up to be fat little eunuchs. Many of them undoubtedly ended up as part of Thanksgiving or Christmas dinners.

Fifty years later at a medical school reunion in St. Louis I met a Dr. Dallas Anthony. He was a radiologist who had graduated from my medical school five years ahead of me and practiced in Springfield, Missouri. I vaguely remembered that name being recorded in my diary and asked Dr. Anthony if he had caponized chicks to earn money for medical school. He grinned knowingly and nodded his head. I then announced that I had been one of his assistants many years earlier.

Even though there was more than enough to do at home my parents didn't discourage me from accepting these outside employment opportunities. Most of the time Paul and I kept the money we earned, but there were critical times we voluntarily put it 'into the pot.' We also bought some of our own clothes. These job experiences made my year out of school go faster and I learned some of the lessons of employee responsibility.

For several weeks that summer our pond went dry. Paul and I hauled water for our cows from Creighton's spring about three hundred yards from our property line. This was laboriously accomplished with a ten-gallon can tied to our wheelbarrow, requiring many daily trips. We were happily relieved when the fall rains filled the pond again.

When the weather got cold we spent many hours cutting enough wood for heating and cooking. Both our axes and our saws were old and difficult to keep sharp enough to cut the oak wood which was our principal fuel. I did a big part of it but Paul pitched in when he was home from school.

Mother made an effort to see that there was time for relaxation. She insisted that I lie down and rest for a while after lunch, and she always saw that there were coffee breaks both morning and afternoon. After we ate supper and participated in our family sing-along, Paul and I retired to the boys' cottage. While he had homework to do, I read myself to sleep with the light from a kerosene lamp. During those long months I read the Bible from cover to cover. Daddy had collected an extensive library, and old National Geographic Magazines were available. One of our neighbors passed on to us their copies of The Saturday Evening Post in which I especially enjoyed the serialized fiction. When Life Magazine was first published in 1930 Mother's brother Roy, in Washington DC, subscribed for us. That was a special horizon-extending treat for our family.

And so that 1937-38 school year passed by without me. On April 7, 1938, we were all delighted with the arrival of our youngest brother David. Ingrid vividly remembers his delivery at home. We were now five sisters and five brothers! That same summer was happily punctuated by the visits of our lively, cheerful Grandma Matilda, plus uncles, aunts and cousins from Nebraska, Iowa and Minnesota. These afforded opportunities to make outings to nearby scenic attractions of the Ozarks.

Mr. Espy, Rogersville High School music teacher, gave me several violin lessons at a nearby rural school. I used an old fiddle passed on to our family by Grandpa Jacobson. In July I was freed up from my home duties to spend three delightful days at the 4-H camp on the James River. All these happy events made that summer slip by a little faster. My diary entry on August 29th reads, "Went to school today! It sure does seem nice to get back after almost two years!" Actually it had only been fifteen months. I was definitely a bit more mature and ready to apply myself to the next big step in my formal education.

GOLDEN WEDDING DAYS

For much of the summer of 1937 we were eagerly anticipating our safari to Grandpa and Grandma Jacobson's Golden Wedding Anniversary celebration in Illinois. I couldn't remember any of our uncles, aunts and cousins on that side of the family. It had been eight years since the grandparents had visited us in Verona. Mother, who was excited about going home again, seemed anxious to show off her nine lively offspring. We didn't know it at the time but she was already carrying little David so he would be making the trip, too.

Daddy had made arrangements for an elderly Swedish couple, the Lundstroms, to stay at our house to tend the chickens and hogs. Mr. Fallon had agreed to let us turn our cows into the pasture with his and see that they got milked.

How do you transport two adults, nine children and their luggage over four hundred miles in one small Chevy sedan? Gustav and Mary sat with Mother in front and the rest of us were layered two and three deep in the back seat. Some of the luggage was loaded on the running boards and the remainder on the floor or in nooks and corners throughout the interior. Years later I was reminded of our overflowing jalopy by the campus competitions to see which fraternity could stuff the most college students in a VW Beetle. My parents would have won hands down if they had entered such a contest.

My diary indicates that we started off at noon on Sept. 29th and headed northeast on Highway 66, America's main street from Chicago to Los Angeles. We were too crowded to read or play games but we could still sing all of our favorite songs. We putted along until well after dark when we stopped near Cuba, Missouri. We were only two-thirds of the way to St. Louis. A festive atmosphere prevailed as we crowded into a rather small tourist cabin. That was the first time in years that we had all slept under one roof. The smaller children slept crossways on double beds and we older ones on the floor. Mother urged us to settle down quietly so Daddy could get his much-needed sleep.

We resumed our journey at four-thirty the following morning and reached 'Saint Looey' at mid-day. That meant that it had taken twenty-four hours to travel the first two hundred and thirty miles. Frequent pit stops reduced miles-per-hour considerably. I was impressed with Daddy's patience. Miraculously there hadn't been any flat tires. The massive grandeur of the buildings in downtown St. Louis was astounding. As we slowly rolled through the big city, people stared and smiled at the mass of humanity packed in our little car. We must have appeared like a real life version of the Beverly Hillbillies. A special dimension of excitement arose as we crossed the mighty 'cafe-au-lait'-colored Mississippi River into Illinois. We piled out of the vehicle for a picnic lunch at the park in a town named Mt. Olive. In Springfield we stopped briefly at the Abraham Lincoln Home. The big anniversary festivities were scheduled in Colona on the following afternoon so we had to keep moving northward. We were exhausted when we reached Grandpa's house at 3:00 AM. Our parents didn't want to disturb the grandparents at that ungodly hour so we parked until they awakened and welcomed us with open arms. When he unfolded and climbed out of the car, sleepy little Carl complained, "My eggs lake!" Grandma fed us breakfast and settled us in various corners of their little retirement home for a few hours rest. My diary says that we slept late.

Paul and I were awakened by a powerful chugging sound. Less than a hundred yards away a thirty-foot boat was slowly approaching on the Hennepin Canal which went right by Grandpa's house. We dressed and hurried out in time to see the lockkeeper directing the vessel into the hydraulic lock. We were amazed to watch him slowly crank the gate which released the water, lowering the boat about ten feet to the next level. The pilot waved at us from his position at the wheel and saluted us with a wonderful blast on his horn as he chugged off toward the Mississippi River. The Hennepin Canal had facilitated a shortcut between the Illinois and Mississippi Rivers for years but was shut down not long after our visit, replaced by railroads and highways.

In the afternoon we all congregated at the town hall which had been rented for the big reception. A huge crowd had gathered both inside and outside the building. Eight uncles and aunts greeted us and we were introduced to eleven cousins. There was concern when Grandpa and Grandma hadn't arrived at the appointed time. An uncle hurried to their house to find Grandma attempting to tie Grandpa's necktie. He didn't wear one often and in the excitement had forgotten the mechanics of tying the knot. Grandma also was baffled but the situation was soon remedied. They were embarrassed as they took their places in the reception line, but soon appeared to be enjoying the well wishes of a host of friends and family. We grandchildren waited somewhat impatiently through that long procession and a series of speeches before what we considered the main event, namely supper. My diary recorded a candid comment that the food was great except for some 'rotten' chicken. In those days of primitive refrigeration it had apparently stood too long before consumption. As far as I know nobody got sick. To make up for the chicken I didn't eat, I treated myself to an extra helping of homemade ice cream.

Grandpa and Grandma must have been exhausted by the time the festivities wound down. I suspect that he couldn't wait to get home, plop down into his easy chair and light his pipe. Grandma was probably counting the minutes until she could get into her bedroom to release the stays of her foundation garment and get into something more comfortable. They both had put on a good show and seemed to revel in the love and adulation of their family and friends.

Grandpa and Grandma had weathered fifty happy, productive, but sometimes difficult years together. At the age of seven he came to Illinois with his family from Varmland, Sweden. During their prolonged voyage on a sailing ship Grandpa remembered the sailors teasing him because he wore leather pants. From his early teens he worked in the coalmines until he had saved enough money to buy a farm. He courted and married Albertina Stoll, a pretty young schoolteacher whose parents also had emigrated from Sweden. Their cooperative efforts created Maplehurst, one of the finest farms in the community. Their five healthy children learned to work hard and excelled both in the classroom and in athletic pursuits.

I was intrigued and somewhat awed by these uncles and aunts whom I was meeting for the first time that I could remember. Uncle Roy, Mother's oldest brother, projected a powerful image. Both he and his wife Dorothy were Phi Beta Kappa graduates of Northwestern University. He was a star pitcher on the university baseball team and quarterbacked the football team until a shoulder injury terminated participation in both sports. As an ardent supporter of President Roosevelt he had been appointed to the National Labor Relations Board, a position he held at the time of the reunion. I wasn't old enough to be aware of it but suspect that his political orientation created some polarization within the family. To me he was a great guy, concerned about everybody on a personal level, with a wide variety of interests. Their son Charles is a brilliant laser scientist and inventor in California's Silicone Valley.

Uncle Bill, the star baseball player, was of course our athletic hero. Now in his forties, he was an awesome specimen who moved with cat-like grace. He watched us young cousins playing ball, picked up a bat and hit the first pitch almost out of sight. He then went over and started pitching horseshoes with his cousin Rolly Stoll. I was enthralled as he pitched one ringer after another. That had become one of his recreational activities during baseball spring training in Florida. In later years he became one of the best horseshoe players in Northern Illinois. Watching him inspired me to become a horseshoe addict and I think I could have given him serious competition.

Easy-going Uncle Verne, the youngest brother, was just a delight for everybody. He was blessed with a wonderful smile and a deep gentle mesmerizing speaking voice which would have projected perfectly on the radio. His brothers insisted that he was the best athlete in the family and could have excelled as a professional baseball player. After a stint in the Navy in WWI he attended Augustana College. He then recognized how much his father needed him on the farm. He courted and married a high school sweetheart Lula Kruse. We all agree that their marriage was 'made in heaven.' They lived on the home farm nearly seventy years raising many tons of corn and other grains, and thousands of hogs. Verne had grown up on the farm spending nearly all of his 90-plus years there. One of his claims to fame was eating pancakes for breakfast, cooked by either Grandma or Aunt Lula, just about every day of his life on the farm. Their daughter Betty possesses many of the neat characteristics of each of her parents. We especially appreciate her efforts to compile historical information about the Jacobson family.

Lula, the final survivor of her generation, died in 1998 at the age of 98. She was a wonderful loving person, the glue which held the entire clan together. A few years ago she sent me a full-sized color poster entitled Hogs Are Beautiful. Two red hogs are shown nuzzling each other affectionately. That treasure is now prominently posted in our garage.

Mother's youngest sister Mae was always special to me. I can still hear her jolly laugh. Like her mother, she became a teacher. She married Clyde Ross and settled in Princeton, Illinois, and raised six bright and handsome children, Howard, Dorothy, Arnold, Carol, Steve and Jon. Uncle Clyde was slender and Daddy was about thirty pounds below his healthy weight in 1937. Somebody made a comment that Mother and Mae had chosen husbands who were quite puny compared with their robust, athletic Jacobson brothers. I was old enough to be incensed because, in those difficult years, I didn't think Daddy was getting enough to eat. Aunt Mae lived well into her nineties and remained alert and outgoing to the end.

During the reunion days Paul and I stayed with Uncle Bill and Aunt Vurl so we became fairly well acquainted with their children. Bill, the oldest, was a freshman at Augustana College and a member of the wrestling team. Carita, an attractive teenager, lit up her surroundings with her sparkling smile and friendly manner. Julian was my senior by only a few months but a head taller. He was already making a name for himself on the high school baseball diamond. Ted, the youngest at that time, was a happy-go-lucky five-year-old. Another brother, Bruce, was born a few months later.

Julian took us on a fish-salvaging expedition in an isolated slough off the Rock River. We literally scooped up at least a hundred small bullhead catfish, brought them home and spent most of the afternoon cleaning them. If we hadn't harvested them they would have died in a short time in their shrinking environment. While he was working away I somehow remember that Julian kept singing, "Night and you, --- and blue Hawaii. --- The night is heavenly --- And you are heaven to me."

Julian had given up his bed for me and slept on the floor. On our last night in Illinois, disaster struck. I had survived all the previous nights but after an exciting day my bedwetting history repeated itself with a vengeance. I was totally mortified to wake up in a warm lake of my own unconscious production. I simply didn't have the courage to confess, hurriedly made the bed, and stuffed my damp nightclothes into my traveling bag. When Mother discovered them it was her turn to be embarrassed. She immediately wrote a letter to Aunt Vurl apologizing for her leaky offspring. I was relieved not to have to face Julian. I didn't see him again for 53 years when we were finally reunited at his home near Eugene, Oregon, in 1990. My apology for saturating his bed in 1937 was accepted and he roared out a typical Jacobson laugh. He had completely forgotten the episode but I most certainly had not! Predictably my diary contains no reference to that mortifying experience. On a sad note, Julian was found dead of a heart attack on a solo fishing trip two years after that Oregon reunion.

Unfortunately, Bill's marriage to Aunt Vurl later disintegrated. We never lost contact with her and she remained a friend to all of us nieces and nephews until she died in her late nineties.

On our last day of wedding anniversary festivities we all attended the Methodist church in Colona. Then we had an exciting picnic day at Grandpa's farm, consolidating our new relationships with uncles, aunts, and cousins. It would be a long time before we could be together again.

Grandpa and Grandma at Home

With their grandchildren.

On Monday the big party came to an end and we headed back to the Ozarks. Mother was going to stay in Colona for a few days and then Grandpa would drive her and the pre-school children home. Daddy was determined that we stop in Rock Island so that we older children could see the campus of Augustana College and

Seminary. He even showed us where he and Mother took their first walks in the park overlooking the Mississippi River. We were introduced to several of his professors and got to meet Marian Gustafson, one of Daddy's lively young cousins, then an Augustana undergraduate.

At the anniversary activities Grandpa Jacobson's older brother Charley had insisted that we stop at his home in Canton on the first night of our homeward journey. He had a surprise for us. Uncle Charley was the most prosperous of his clan. He started as an adolescent laboring underground, mining coal, and ended up owning two productive mines. But what kind of a surprise awaited us at his house? After our stop in Rock Island we didn't arrive at Uncle Charley's until eight o'clock at night. We crawled wearily out of the little Chevy, were warmly welcomed, fed and put to bed. In the morning after breakfast Uncle Charley took us out to his garage and opened the door. There stood a huge shiny black sedan in mint condition. The axles had been jacked up and mounted on blocks. It was the biggest passenger automobile I had ever seen. Uncle Charley said, "This is my 1927 Packard. It has only traveled 5,000 miles and I am no longer able to drive. I have been trying to decide what to do with it. The other day when I saw your big family crammed into such a small car I knew what I wanted to see happen to this old monster. Please accept it as a gift from me."

Daddy was flabbergasted and insisted that it was much too valuable a gift to be giving us. His protests were deflected, and so we came into possession of a marvelous traveling machine. The large space between front and back seats contained two small removable chairs. And there was far more room for luggage than in the Chevy.

Much of that day was consumed dismounting the car from blocks, pumping up the tires and checking all systems. We didn't get on the road until 4:00 PM. We were delighted at all the interior space and excited to be sailing along in such elegance. Daddy was a conservative driver, but on a straight stretch of highway couldn't resist the temptation to 'open up the throttle.' When the speedometer reached 65 MPH he cautiously slowed down. After staying overnight in a tourist cabin in Jacksonville, Illinois, we loaded up to continue our safari, but our wonderful new automobile refused to start. We had either purchased bad gasoline or there may have been condensed water in the tank. Uncle Charley had told Daddy what to do under such circumstances. On the to do under such circumstances. On the engine block six thimble-sized cups were mounted over the cylinder heads. By putting a few drops of gasoline in each of them and turning a valve, fuel would drip into the cylinders near the spark plugs. Daddy followed those instructions and sure enough, the old Packard gave a mighty roar and carried us on our way.

When we reached the outskirts of St. Louis I marveled at Daddy's ability to calmly negotiate the fast-moving bumper-to-bumper traffic. I doubted that I would ever have the courage to get behind the wheel of a vehicle in such conditions. (Little did I know what I'd have to face on Los Angeles freeways sixty years later.) After a brief visit to Concordia Lutheran Seminary we drove to beautiful Forest Park where we had a picnic lunch. Then we were treated to an exciting visit to the famous St. Louis Zoo. We children were especially entranced by the performance of the trained chimpanzees. Daddy seemed enthralled to be in the presence of the wonderful wild animals of Africa again. I think he would have hung around longer if he hadn't realized that we had to get home that night. We finally broke away from the zoo at 4:00 PM and headed southwest on Highway 66. With less cramped seating we children slept much of the way to Springfield. We arrived back at Bethany Homestead at midnight.

We were up early the next morning. Ingrid, eleven, and Veda, nine, were the little mothers of the household in Mother's absence. They had to rush to get ready to go to school with Eunice and Carl. Paul hurried off, walking the mile to catch the bus to Rogersville High School. This of course was my year out of school and one of my first responsibilities was to retrieve our four cows from Fallon's farm. Since our pond was dry I had to haul water for all the animals from Creighton's spring in ten-gallon cans balanced on the wheelbarrow.

Five days later, on October 12th, Grandpa Jacobson arrived from Illinois, with Mother, Martha, Gustav and Mary. We were excited to be all together again. Ingrid remembers how much younger and happier Mother looked after this special time with her family. Two days later Daddy went back to Illinois with Grandpa to retrieve our old Chevy. When he returned it was parked near the house and often used by the younger children as an extra room for reading, playing, and napping.

In later years we older children still enjoy sharing memories of those exciting days of our trip to our grandparents' golden wedding anniversary. For me it was definitely one of the highlights of growing up in the Ozarks.

BACK TO SCHOOL - 1938

After 15 months out of school I was tremendously excited about beginning my four years of high school at Rogersville.

On the first day of school Paul and I were still working for Mr. Fallon so we had to get up at 4:00 AM and milk his cows. We then returned home and milked our own. After a breakfast of hot cornmeal cereal, coffee, and toast, we got dressed. In the meantime Mother prepared our lunch, four thick-sliced sandwiches for each of us, made with her wonderful homemade bread. Two were made with generous slices of meatloaf and two with peanut butter. The brown bag also contained a ripe tomato with a little packet of salt and a bright red Jonathon apple.

We were scheduled to catch the school bus at 7:30. In 1938 it picked us up just a mile north of our house. (The following year it was one-and-a-half miles west.) As we hurried toward the bus stop Paul gave me some helpful suggestions. As the orange wooden cracker-box bus of ancient vintage, with a capacity of 30 students, rolled to a stop in front of us my heart was pounding. The friendly bus driver, Clay Litrell, Rogersville's town barber, invited us to climb aboard. I stepped up, glanced over the noisy mass of humanity in the bus and didn't see a single familiar face. Paul didn't introduce me so I was on my own. Seating consisted of a long bench on each side so that we faced the center and couldn't easily avoid looking at each other. I plopped down on the nearest available space. One of the upper classmen said, "So you're Paul's little brother. He's sure a lot better looking than you are!" That didn't do much for my self-esteem. I wished that I had possessed the chutzpah to say, "So what! I'm smarter than he is!" But I was living with the reality that I was a homely redheaded freckle-faced shrimp with bad teeth, at least a head shorter than my handsome big brother.

At the next stop I was pleased to see my friend Glen Pursley from our 4-H club climb aboard. Our bus stop was located 15 miles from Rogersville so there was ample visiting time. The next four years afforded many happy hours sharing the good and the bad times with friends. I thought the long bus ride might provide some study time but soon gave that up. A few of the upper class guys and gals were paired off as couples. Overt amorous behavior was not acceptable in those days. Handholding was about as far as anybody dared venture in displaying affection. I was too timid and insecure to try anything like that during my four years at Rogersville.

Some of the older boys tested the patience of our bus driver with a trick with which he was obviously familiar. They got all of us to rock back and forth with our hands joined across the middle aisle. Soon the body of the bus was swaying back and forth alarmingly. Mr. Litrell immediately pulled over to the side of the road and angrily declared, "There will be no more of that nonsense!" He then told the story of the bus in another district which had been rolled over by just the same shenanigans we had been pulling. In that accident several students had been seriously injured.

After a 40-minute ride we arrived at the tiny town of Rogersville. At the high school, all forty freshmen were assembled in the study hall and registration was completed. I had some explaining to do when I responded, "Tanganyika, in East Africa," to the place-of-birth question. One of my new classmates was asked the same question, "And where were you born, Jimmy?" In all seriousness he replied, "In our parlor!"

We freshmen were awed by our principal George Riley. He was at least 6 feet 4 inches and reminded me of Abraham Lincoln without the beard. He related well to both faculty and students. As a coach he had led several basketball teams into the state championship tournament. A highlight of the freshman year was his citizenship class which covered a wide range of important issues. Not knowing names he identified students by their physical characteristics. In 1936 my brother Paul was a freshman in Mr. Riley's famous class. Paul was trying unsuccessfully to slick his hair down after a summer of Daddy's short crew cuts. Mr. Riley wanted to ask him a question and said, "Hey, you little porcupine with the hair sticking straight up! What are the characteristics of a good citizen?" Paul's friends started calling him 'Porky,' short for 'porcupine' and that name stuck with him for the next four years. When I came along I became 'Little Porky.' In one of our early sessions Mr. Riley called on me asking "What do you want to be when you grow up?" I replied, "I really like vocal music, and I'm also enjoying vocational agriculture." Mr. Riley responded in his deep Ozarkian drawl, "Well, it sounds as if you are on the way to becoming a singing farmer." He challenged us to think seriously about what we were going to do with our lives and talents.

One day in the boys' restroom one of my freshman buddies made some highly uncomplimentary remarks about an offensive odor which was emanating from one of the enclosed stalls. I couldn't help laughing aloud at that pungent commentary. We couldn't see the occupant until he stood up, and guess who? — Mr. Riley looked down at us over the top of the stall! We were absolutely horrified until our distinguished principal gave a sheepish grin and said, "Sorry about that, guys. I just can't help it." Our little school district couldn't afford separate 'johns' for students and faculty.

Another person whom I soon learned to admire and respect was our elderly custodian, Mr. Jack Delzell. In addition to keeping the building clean and comfortable, he was a friend to everybody. We freshmen soon learned that he was a sympathetic listener who always had time to give an encouraging word and a pat on the back. Many times I remember going out of the way at noon or between classes just to have a few moments with him. He may not have been formally educated but he was a wise counselor. The faculty recognized and respected his unique and wholesome qualities. I'm sure that he originally sought this job because he enjoyed being around young people. And the feeling was mutual!

THREE SPECIAL FRIENDS

Once I entered high school my horizons expanded as new friends came into my life. Gratification came from friendly upper class students, some of whom took me under their wings and helped me make the transition from a one-room rural elementary school mentality. Most of all I enjoyed a happy camaraderie with my fellow freshmen.

Of course other older students asserted their dominant status and did their part to keep us in our places. One obnoxious sophomore on our bus was constantly needling me with insulting gibes. One morning he lit a fuse that led to a violent explosion. In a loud voice he sneeringly asserted, "You're so ugly that when you were born your mother threw away the baby and raised the afterbirth!" I was especially incensed at the implied insult to my parents. From a friend I might have shrugged it off but he wasn't just kidding. He was bigger than I was but I didn't hesitate in my attack. In a few moments I had wrestled him down off his seat and pounded his head on the floor a couple of times. The driver stopped the bus and yelled, "You two break it up or you're both going to be walking!" My adversary never tormented me again and I seemed to gain a little respect from the rest of the crowd. There were no repercussions and I was grateful to my big brother for not reporting the incident at home.

Early on, I forged a special friendship with the Freeman brothers. John and Tom were fraternal twins who didn't even look like siblings. Tom stood over six feet tall with a powerful physique and John was a little shrimp like me. They were second oldest offspring of a large family which scratched a meager living from a hardscrabble rocky farm near Rogersville. As far as I know they were the first members of their clan to attend high school and they were determined to take full advantage of this golden opportunity.

Tom and John were intensely devoted to their parents. I stayed overnight with the Freemans on several occasions when afterschool activities kept me from riding home on the bus. Their mother more or less adopted me as one of the brood. Her warm nurturing qualities were clearly reflected in her children. At one of the early school open houses I was impressed with the manner in which the twins treated their father. He was a quiet unsophisticated man dressed in bib overalls, with a colorful Ozarkian accent. Tom and John were obviously proud of him. They led him through classrooms, introduced him to their teachers and classmates, and happily showed him what they were doing in the vocational agriculture shop. At that stage it seemed that most of us tended to shy away from our parents in public, but not the Freeman twins. Their relationship with their mother and father reminded me of accounts of Abraham Lincoln's devotion to his stepmother, Sarah Bush Lincoln.

John and I were kindred spirits who thoroughly enjoyed spending time together. After I received high marks on our first classroom tests he frequently flattered me with a barrage of questions. On the other hand, I recognized that he had special skills and insights that I envied. For one thing he had a touch of mechanical genius and could fix just about anything. Tom shared this talent. They brought an old broken-down horse-drawn grain binder into the Ag shop. It was a complicated piece of machinery but after tearing it down they reconstructed it piece by piece. And it worked! The twins complemented each other nicely. Both brothers were kind and understanding and I can't remember them saying anything derogatory about anybody.

One vivid memory reminds me of Tom's awesome physical power. Somebody had brought two pairs of big padded 16-ounce boxing gloves to school. Tom and I put them on and were playfully sparring around. I didn't think he was very fast and was dancing about, trying to get in a few punches. Suddenly he unleashed a powerful right hand which caught me square on the chin and knocked me cold. I don't know how long I was out but the next thing I remember was Tom hovering over me. There was concern in his eyes as he said, "I didn't mean to hit you that hard, John!" That was the last time I ever put on boxing gloves.

One day at the end of our freshman year the whole school received a terrible shock. The final period was over and we were climbing into our busses for our homeward journey. A big black hearse drove up and stopped at the school entrance in plain sight of the whole student body. Mr. Farrel, the undertaker, hurried to the bus which the Freeman boys were entering. He had the awful responsibility of informing them that he had just come from their home where their father had died of a heart attack. We could actually see the body through the window of the hearse. The Freemans had no telephone so this was the only way Mr. Farrel could catch my friends. Mr. Freeman was not yet 40 years old. Our class attended the funeral as a group and many of us shed tears with the family. I had never before experienced a death in the family of close friends and was profoundly moved.

That was the first of a tragic sequence of deaths in the Freeman family. While we were still in high school their oldest brother died of an apparent coronary. Tom himself suffered the same fate soon after he and John graduated from the University of Missouri with degrees in agricultural engineering.

I only saw Tom Freeman twice after our graduation. In February, 1943, he was a handsome but formidable-looking MP stationed at Ft. Leavenworth, Kansas when I was being inducted into the army. We had a couple of meals together in the mess hall and he gave me some good pointers which were helpful in surviving basic training. The last time I saw him was at the University of Missouri in 1948 when I was courting my future wife Louise, also a student there. I stayed overnight with him and his new bride and had a wonderful visit. Two years later I was shocked by the news of his fatal illness.

Finally another younger brother, Delbert, expired with the same diagnosis. All died before their fortieth birthdays. By then it had been determined that they were victims of an inherited disease known as Beta-hyperlipoproteinemia which clogs the arteries at an accelerated rate. John and his younger brother Jack were the only surviving male members of the Freeman family. Each was the smaller brother of a much larger fraternal twin and has lived on with dietary restrictions and medical treatment. The female members of the family were unaffected and their mother lived into her nineties.

Glen Pursley was another special friend. He and I had had many good experiences in our years in the 4-H club. We had worked together on dairy judging and demonstration teams and enjoyed studying together in high school. His father was a dairy farmer with a fine herd of Guernseys. Glen went on to earn a PhD in dairy husbandry and had a fine career as a consultant at the state level. Glen and his son also developed a prize-winning herd of Holstein dairy cattle.

Following in my brother Paul's footsteps, I briefly experimented with cigarette smoking. Glen caught me in the act and really scolded me. I was already disgusted with myself and told him that if he ever saw me smoking again or heard that I had, I would owe him ten dollars. That was the end of that nasty habit and I was grateful to Glen for shaming me out of it.

Glen's mother was one of my favorite adults during my adolescence. Many years later I paid her a surprise visit at the Pursley farm. She was over 90 and hadn't seen me for 50 years but immediately recognized me and called me by name as soon as I walked into the room. Glen's wife worked with Dr. Dallas Anthony, the Springfield radiologist whom I had assisted caponizing male chicks when he was a premed student and I was barely into my teens. Just before I retired I met an attractive secretary named Ruth Pursley at Denver Children's Hospital. Her accent seemed hauntingly familiar and I soon discovered that she was Glen's daughter. I also admired and appreciated Glen's older brother Ray who was another fine dairy farmer.

John, Glen, and I were last together at our 50th class reunion and spent a delightful exciting evening catching up on each other's lives and times. John and I also brought our 90-year-old mothers together for some memorable moments of reminiscence. They recalled certain embarrassing anecdotes which we had forgotten about our youthful foibles.

"LEARNING TO DO, DOING TO LEARN"

Vocational agriculture with membership in the Future Farmers Of America was offered as a four-year work-study program at our high school for the first time while I was a freshman in 1938. The Department of Health, Education and Welfare sponsors the FFA organization nationally. Young men are trained to be better farmers, good citizens, and leaders in the community. Our official motto was: "Learning to do, Doing to learn, Earning to live, Living to serve." And the national slogan was "The Successful Farmer of Tomorrow is the Future Farmer of Today."

A fine building, complete with manual arts shop, had been finished in time for the opening day of school. Members of the school board considered themselves fortunate to have hired young Mr. W.O. Barrow as the first teacher. He had turned down the opportunity to teach at the University of Missouri because he wanted to 'be where the action was.' He was to become my favorite high school teacher and a life-long friend, along with his warm and caring wife Mary.

Although the frustrations of our one-horse agriculture at Bethany Homestead in drought years hadn't convinced me to pursue farming, I signed up for the course. Very soon I developed a real fascination for the material to which we were introduced. We were really getting involved with many facets of the basic essence of life itself. Mr. Barrow was not an eloquent lecturer but he knew his material well. Considering the fact that we were immature and mischievous adolescents he managed to hold our attention most of the time. The fact that he cared for each of us on a personal level helped to keep us focused on what he said. When things got out of hand he could effectively lay down the law, too.

He also was blessed with a great sense of humor and laughed often and heartily. On one occasion I was amused to see him stifle a laugh when he really wanted to guffaw with his students. We were at the end of the classroom period during which we had been studying some of the basic facts of cattle breeding. We were preparing to go from the classroom into the shop to work on our manual arts projects. One of my naughtier classmates had discovered that the green heavy-duty hand soap used in our shop made a wonderful substitute for modeling clay. He surreptitiously created a life-sized replica of the male reproductive organs of a well-endowed bull and mounted it on a table so as to be plainly visible when we filed into the shop. About a dozen of us had walked through the door into the shop ahead of Mr. Barrow. We spotted the prodigious life-like work of art and were roaring with laughter when our teacher discovered the object of our attention. I distinctly saw him start to laugh but abruptly put on an unhappy face. He declared that he wouldn't tolerate that sort of nonsense. The school board wouldn't have either and would have held him personally responsible. But I clearly saw that flickering instant when he wished that he could have laughed with us. The offensive object was mashed into one big ball and returned to the large soap container to be used only for it's intended purpose. As far as I know Mr. Barrow didn't pursue the identity of the culprit. He probably had strong suspicions. None of us ever tested his patience again with that brand of humor. He probably went home that day and told Mary that he had had to put up with a 'lot of bull' from his freshman class. Fifty years later I was reunited with Tom Lewis, the perpetrator of this misadventure, in California. He neither remembered the event nor did he deny that he might have done it.

Mr. Barrow was a 'chicken man.' He had to 'cover the waterfront' in his teaching but he was particularly knowledgeable in poultry or fowl husbandry. Eggs provided the principal source of income at our little farm so it was appropriate that I chose our Leghorn chickens as my vocational agriculture project. We spent time in class developing balanced diets for laying hens, preventing infections, etc. Mr. Barrow was a serious student of poultry diseases and parasites. When a chicken in our flock died he urged us to bring it to class for an autopsy. It was by no means a pleasant chore to help him cut open a smelly dead chicken, but this was serious business. Our teacher could more often than not find the cause of death while teaching us a little anatomy and surgery. I didn't know it but I was getting some basic science indoctrination which would be helpful in a few years in medical school.

Mr. Barrow was a whiz at poultry judging, which is both a science and an art. He could accurately identify the hens which laid the most eggs. Under his tutelage student poultry-judging teams did well in contests against other schools. I was on our Rogersville team one year but never felt that I had the knack of picking out the most productive chickens. After I graduated, one of Mr. Barrow's teams won the Missouri State and the National vocational agriculture poultry-judging contest. That was a big thrill for both him and his students.

An urgent agricultural problem in the Ozarks had been created by tilling methods which permitted rapid soil erosion. Mr. Barrow emphasized that half of the topsoil in our region had already been washed away in the relatively few years it had been plowed. He taught us the benefits of crop rotation to improve the soil and limit erosion. Contour plowing and terracing could save much of the soil which up-and-down-the-hill cultivation permitted to run off with the rains. Except for the river bottoms the Ozarks had only a thin rocky layer of rather poor soil from which life and livelihood originated.

We were taught procedures for testing the soil. Alfalfa, a wonderful high-protein crop, was grown infrequently in the Ozarks because the soil was too acid. This could be corrected with the application of lime. Mr. Barrow taught methods and techniques which were revolutionary for backwoods farmers. But their sons went home from school with these new strategies, which slowly and gradually caught on. Now, sixty years later, the countryside has been transformed into a much more prosperous productive agricultural region. Mr. Barrow, along with agricultural extension agents and 4-H club leaders, had had much to do with this remarkable progress.

FUTURE FARMERS OF AMERICA

Most of the 60-plus boys taking vocational agriculture at Rogersville High School joined the Future Farmers of America organization. Each student was required to conduct a specific supervised agricultural project in addition to the daily classroom and manual arts shop instruction. We were encouraged to exhibit our animals and crops in local and State fairs, but my chickens were not of a caliber to consider that option. Several of our members had purebred cattle, sheep, and hogs which won their share of ribbons. These livestock often formed a nucleus of successful farming ventures for their young owners after they got out of school.

My brother Paul was elected as the first president of our FFA chapter for its first two years, and I succeeded him through the next two years. Mr. Barrow once asked me, "Don't you have another brother ready for high school to take over the 'Hult Dynasty'?" We conducted regular meetings and participated in a variety of activities. Mr. Barrow insisted that we conduct these sessions according to Robert's Rules of Order for parliamentary procedure. We even had contests with other chapters to determine who could present the most orderly and meaningful business meeting.

On one occasion several of us presented a half-hour informational radio program about the FFA on a Springfield station. After Mr. Barrow's introductory remarks we each briefly described the projects with which we were personally involved. With guidance from our music teacher, four of us worked up a boy's quartet which sang at the beginning and end of our broadcast. Our stage fright resulted in a pretty awful performance. That didn't keep our parents from expressing proud appreciation.

We even had our own FFA basketball teams. None of the varsity squad was eligible so it amounted to an intramural function and everyone who wished to play was allowed to participate. Mr. Barrow set up a few games against the 'Aggies' from nearby high schools. We weren't any good and I can't remember winning a single game, but we had a great time. I was a terrible player and became a marginal member of the FFA second team. I specialized in an awkward jump shot which rarely came near to the basket. My athletic friends said that it was comical to watch me launch my missiles. Every time I got the ball they would yell, "Shoot, shoot, shoot!" When I did they had a good laugh. They called me 'Jump Shot Hult.'

We had a penchant for giving each other nicknames. I have told you that one of my FFA mates dubbed me 'Little Porky' because my big brother Paul was known as just plain 'Porky.' Then one day we were discussing the finer points of dairy cattle judging. A student asked Mr. Barrow, "What is the ideal color for the Guernsey breed?" Our professor hesitated then fixed his eyes on my bright red hair. "That's it," he said. "Just take a look at John's hair and you have it." Thereafter I became 'Guernsey Hult.' In spite of my small size my upper body muscles were well developed from all my wood chopping. I discovered that I could put a belt around my chest, take in a deep breath, contract my muscles and rip it apart. One day a friend was wearing a heavy-duty belt he had just received as a birthday present. He said, "I bet you can't tear this one apart, John!" I accepted the challenge and gave it my best shot. When he saw the leather begin to tear he shouted, "Hold it, hold it. You win!" After that I was known as 'Beltbuster.' At a weekend summer FFA camp with four other high schools we had a contest to see who could swim the farthest underwater. I could hold my breath a long time and surfaced well ahead of my nearest competitor. For a time thereafter I became 'Submarine Hult.' Other nicknames are best not mentioned.

During my senior year our chapter had a Halloween party. Mr. Barrow must have thought that would keep us from such naughty activities as tipping over privies and other juvenile mischief. We decorated the shop with corn shocks, pumpkins, etc., and created a slide so everybody would have to enter through a window. School dances were not permitted in those days, but music was provided with a phonograph playing the old scratchy 78 RPM records. Group party games did not include 'Spin-the-Bottle.' That suggestion had been unequivocally vetoed by higher authority. Refreshments included cider (definitely unfermented) and donuts. Most participants considered the evening a success.

That wild party was the occasion of my first date. I had a powerful crush on an attractive gal in the junior class. We mimeographed our invitations, rolled them up, and inserted them into hollowed-out corncobs. I hesitated and nearly backed out several times before getting up enough courage to deliver my white corncob to that special lady. I was delighted that she accepted but sensed a certain lack of enthusiasm. On the big night I was given permission to drive our old 1927 Chevy sedan. Accompanied by a buddy I proudly drove over the Ozark hills to pick up our dates. I thought she was the prettiest girl at the party but my relationship with her was totally platonic for the duration of the evening. She soon began dating a handsome basketball player but remained friendly and kind to me. I haven't seen her since graduation and none of my friends seem to know what happened to her.

Mr. Barrow did more to prepare me for what lay ahead of me in the medical profession than any other high school teacher. Had he chosen that career he would have been a terrific doctor. He instilled into his students a special brand of intellectual curiosity to identify problems and then to find solutions. Even more importantly he demonstrated that he really cared about each one of us personally. He was likewise concerned about our animals and about our fragile farmland environment which needed protection and nurturing. I consider those four years of vocational agriculture and FFA participation under his friendly tutelage one of the most important segments of my formative years.

Future Farmers of America, 50th Anniversary, May, 1988. Myself and Mr. Barrow with special friends: Glen Pursley and John Freeman.

In the winter of 1988 I traveled by Greyhound bus from Colorado to Missouri for the 50th anniversary of the founding of the FFA chapter at Rogersville High School. The current vocational ag teacher gave us a concise update of the current program which had changed dramatically. Many of the students owned prize saddle horses. The most revolutionary development was the switch to coeducational classes. The young women students looked snappy in their blue FFA jackets. Wow! I was fifty years too early. On the other hand I would have had difficulty in concentrating in class. When Mr. Barrow got up to receive special recognition I was impressed that he looked and acted younger than many of his former students in attendance.

FFA SUMMER CAMP, 1941

For most of our teen-aged FFA-members summers were filled with unrelieved dawn-to-dusk work on our family farms. There was little time for recreation. Mr. Barrow and his fellow vocational agriculture teachers from four Webster County high schools agreed that their students should get away for a weekend of pure fun and games. Approximately a hundred of us from Rogersville, Seymour, Elkland and Marshfield gathered at Camp Arrowhead north of Springfield the weekend of August 1-3, 1941. The complex consisted of rustic log cabins, a mess hall, and recreation facilities which included a crystal clear lake with a roped-off swimming area. A beautiful Ozark creek meandered through the woods along one edge of the complex. The only adults on hand were our four teachers and a paid cook.

Each student was asked to bring the following:
Two blankets and toilet articles.
$1.00 for enrollment, wages for the cook, ice, and other expenses.
One dressed chicken (2 lb. or over).
Twelve average sized potatoes.
Six ears of corn.
Six tomatoes.
Six eggs.
One pint of milk.
One pint of jelly or one quart of canned fruit.
(I believe the four teachers provided the bread: It would have taken quite a few loaves to soak up 50-100 pints of jelly.)

One boy from each high school had been appointed to each of five committees and we took our responsibilities seriously. The Registration and Finance Committee enrolled participants, collected fees, paid bills, and assigned cabins. The Food Committee collected and sorted all the food, and helped the cook prepare it. The Mess Hall Committee set up a roster to wait on tables and wash dishes. I was appointed to the Program Committee which planned the daily schedule with guidance of the teachers. We even had a Disciplinary Committee which seemed to be made up of the biggest, strongest, and most imposing guys from each school. Our Rogersville representative was my good friend, big Tom Freeman. That committee didn't have much to do. They did have to arbitrate a disagreement between a couple of the freshman campers.

Our time was totally occupied starting with breakfast at 6:00 AM. Mealtime was a bit chaotic but everybody was eventually served and we consumed vast quantities of food. Dishwashing was the least desirable chore but we each had just one turn.

After breakfast and lunch an hour was designated for free time. Even at that point in my life I felt the need of getting away for a quiet time by being completely alone for a short period. I walked through the forest along the creek adjoining the camp and discovered a nice shallow pool in which a large bass was guarding the eggs in a nest scooped out in the sand. For a half hour I sat on the bank fascinated by this diligent parent chasing away other fish, insuring that its offspring at least got out of the nest. At the end of the hour a bell rang and I hurried back to camp.

During the following hour most of the group played softball or tennis. I wasn't skilled at either so joined the smaller group on the horseshoe courts. I was just learning to throw ringers with some regularity and those three days intensified my life-long addiction to that recreational pursuit. The most important skill is learning how to hold your mouth when you release the shoe. My friends told me that I have a unique mouth set, but unfortunately it doesn't always produce ringers. Nearly 60 years later I still hold my mouth that way.

By far the most popular camp activity was swimming, especially in the heat of August in the Ozarks. Most of us had never been in a bona fide swimming pool, and had learned to swim in local ponds creeks and rivers. At camp we were not allowed to go in the water except at designated hours. We were divided into pairs where each of us was responsible to be aware constantly of the whereabouts of his partner. When a whistle was blown we had to immediately prove our proximity to each other.

On Saturday all who wished lined up for a fifty-yard swimming race across the lake to the rope barrier. At least fifty boys lined up and Mr. Barrow functioned as the starter. At his signal we were off splashing pell-mell through the water. Not one of us had ever had a swimming lesson so there was quite a variety of strokes. Most of us tried to emulate Johnny Weissmuller of Tarzan movie fame. And wonder-of-wonders, I won the race, a real boost to my ego because many of the contestants were superior athletes and I was considered a klutzy bookworm. All that practice in the muddy pond and the James River finally paid off.

The lights in our cabins were turned out at 10:00 PM. But darkness didn't bring silence. There were some lively discussions mostly about girls and cars. One of my cabin mates was also a gifted ghost story teller. For the most part we were so tired physically that we soon went to sleep. I distinctly remember the plaintive call of a whip-poor-will before I drifted off.

Each night after supper we had delightful outdoor campfire sessions. A couple of talented campers had brought their guitars which led to some spirited group singing. One of the teachers told some fascinating and humorous stories.

On Sunday morning many of our parents came to share the day with us. One of the Dads conducted an informal worship service. In those days and in that place we didn't worry about separation of church and state. We were almost 100% Protestant Christians.

For me those three days was a time of complete relaxation, making new friends and generating happy memories for the darker days of Pearl Harbor and World War II which were soon to follow.

"YOU RUN FAST, JOHN, BUT TOO LONG IN THE SAME PLACE!"

Most boys in their teens have Walter Mitty dreams of becoming great athletes. I was no exception, but those fantasies never materialized at Rogersville High School. That failure wasn't because of a lack of effort. I simply didn't have the speed afoot, the reflexes, the coordination, or the aggressive competitiveness to be a real athlete.

There was considerable enthusiasm for sports at our small school. We were disappointed that we didn't have football. Many high schools of our size fielded eight-man teams. Our school board insisted that our district was too poor to make the initial investment for equipment and stadium construction.

Women's sports were definitely underemphasized, the only varsity options being volleyball, softball and tennis. Our girls sometimes played their interscholastic volleyball during the halftime of the boy's basketball games. And they were good, winning league championships regularly. Our women's softball teams were even more successful, but they didn't receive the publicity or emphasis they deserved.

Rogersville had established a fine basketball tradition. Mr. Riley was an excellent coach and his teams often won the Altitude League championship. Basketball was an entirely different game fifty years ago with center jumps after each score and a much slower pace. One of our most successful teams averaged only 34 points per game. It wasn't unusual for teams to score less than a 20-point total for all four quarters. In my sophomore year our team advanced to the Missouri State high school tournament for smaller schools. Our freshman center Marvin Smith towered over most of the competition at 6'5". In one league game he poured in an astounding 31 points. In the first round of the state tournament he was effectively double-teamed so we lost that game. Our star forward, Wayne Lemasters, went on to make the All-State team.

The following year we had great expectations for our basketball team. Early in the season we had an important home game. On that morning I was given permission to drive our old Chevy to school. A block away I stopped to pick up my hero, Wayne Lemasters. He jumped on the running-board and off we roared through town. I didn't slow down enough as I turned into the school driveway and Wayne was thrown off, hitting his head on the pavement. He was briefly unconscious and had a bad headache for an hour or so. I was terribly anxious, first for his welfare and then for how his potential absence would affect the outcome of the big game.

My name would have been mud if he hadn't quickly recovered and played one of his best games, dominating the opposing team that night. Our team didn't get back in the state tournament that year but had a solid winning season. By our senior year Mr. Riley had moved on to a larger high school. Mr. Hamilton the new superintendent took over the team and achieved a winning season with 20 victories and 14 losses.

Forty-eight years later the Rogersville team finally won their first state championship. That great moment occurred just a few days before I attended the 50th anniversary of our FFA chapter in 1988 and they were still celebrating when I arrived. A grandson of one of my classmates was on that team.

I knew that I had no shot at being a varsity basketball player but hoped that I might have a chance to be on the softball team. I soon discovered that I couldn't hit a fast pitch, run to first base rapidly enough, or field a hot grounder. Aside from that I thought I was pretty good! When the coach picked his squad he somehow overlooked me, so I had to search for gratification elsewhere.

Well then, how about trying out for the track team? In our senior year our coach John Hutter lined us up and timed us in the 100-yard dash. Just about everybody finished ahead of me. Maybe I could do better in the distance races? Again I finished way back in the pack in the half-mile and one-mile tryouts. Mr. Hutter smiled at my efforts and said, "John, you really run fast. The only problem is that you run too long in the same place!" He then suggested that I see how I could perform in the weight events, shot-put and discus-throw. After intensive practice heaving heavy rocks at home, I surprised myself with the ability to toss the 12-pound metal ball up to 40 feet. With Mr. Hutter's coaching I learned to hurl the discus over 120 feet. That was better than anybody else on our crew and earned me a spot on our team. Today's high school competitors would laugh at those puny marks. In the interscholastic track meets that spring I actually scored more points for our team than any of our runners. That helped my ego a bit and I was delighted when informed that I had gained a varsity letter. That meant that I could become a member of the 'R' Club! Wow! However, becoming a member of that distinguished fraternity entailed going through a brutal initiation.

The awful night arrived. The most dreaded ordeal involved running a gauntlet of previous initiates wielding paddles carved out of one-inch boards. Some of them had holes drilled through them to intensify the inflicted pain. They even permitted graduates from previous years to participate. I was horrified when I saw the length of the double line of burly paddle wielders. There had to be at least thirty of them. I gritted my teeth and entered torture alley. Somehow I managed to get through without crying out. The awful sound of every board smacking against my tender anatomy was almost as terrible as the mounting throbbing pain. I am convinced that the notorious practice of present-day U.S. Marines of pinning wings through the skin of the chest would have been less painful than what we endured. Other less agonizing but humiliating indignities were heaped upon us. I survived and was duly declared a member of 'R' Club.

For the next two weeks my backside from waist to mid-thigh was black and blue with paddle marks clearly imprinted. My discoloration slowly faded to a brilliant rainbow of greens and yellows. I was careful not to exhibit my bruises to my family, but Mother seemed anxious about the way I was limping around the first few days. My co-initiates showed me that their marks of valor were just as bad as mine.

Our first-year principal insisted on being in attendance because he had heard disturbing rumors about this infamous rite of passage. Forty years later when I visited Mr. Hamilton he told me how upset he had been at the proceedings of that painful evening. He told me that he had overheard a couple of basketball players indicate how they were really going to lay it on that 'bookworm' Hult. As he watched the violence, Mr. Hamilton had feared that there might be serious injuries. His concerns were soon communicated to the school board who saw to it that subsequent initiations were modified considerably. The 'R' Club members objected saying, "We went through it, why shouldn't they?" They were over-ruled.

My athletic ambitions weren't totally squelched yet. I was big enough and strong enough to think that I might be able to play football at Southwest Missouri State Teachers College in the fall of 1942. When I stopped to think of all of my responsibilities at home plus the need to ride my bicycle five miles to and from the campus, reality effectively erased my dream. I still wonder what would have happened if I had at least tried. My friends charitably suggested that I wasn't mean enough to have been a good football player. Oh well, there were still those horseshoes to pitch behind the barn!

MUSIC—MUSIC—MUSIC!

Music played a special role in rounding out my good experiences through four years in high school. The budget for the music department was limited and our instruments weren't particularly good but there was no shortage of enthusiasm.

Before I started my freshman year Rogersville's music director, Mr. George Espy had heard that we had a violin in our house and offered to give me summer lessons. We had inherited this instrument from Grandpa Jacobson and Mother was particularly anxious that one of us should learn to play.

Once a week during that summer Mr. Espy picked up Paul, who was learning to play the trombone, and me with my fiddle. He drove us to a centrally located rural grade school and gave us lessons for 25 cents apiece. Four other students also participated so our teacher was kept busy that afternoon.

Mr. Espy was not a violin player but he knew the basics. I remembered the beautiful sounds which Grandpa drew out of that instrument, but couldn't even come close to duplicating them. My hand-eye coordination was awful but I made enough progress over the summer that I was invited to play second fiddle in the high school orchestra. Our parents were encouraging, but I remember my siblings putting their hands over their ears when I started to practice. I was particularly envious of our virtuoso Charles Lemasters who won the state contest twice as a violin soloist. I knew that I would never excel as a fiddler, but I went on with the orchestra for four years.

After I graduated, Grandpa's violin was passed on to my younger brothers, Carl and Gustav. Both of them soon passed up my skill level. Many years later in Colorado our daughter Martha inherited the instrument and made good progress with a fine teacher named Mr. Iacobuchi. She was eventually selected as concertmistress for the Aurora Youth Symphony. Later she switched from classical violin to old time fiddling, just like her great-grandfather had played it.

In my sophomore year Mr. Espy asked me to play the tuba and I took a crash course under his tutelage. I wasn't at all accomplished but added my 'Oom-pah-pah' to the band throughout the school year. The following year the new music teacher badly needed another trombone. Since Paul had graduated, his instrument was available and I was asked to take over. Paul coached me during the summer and I became a trombone player for my last two years of high school. I wasn't good enough to be asked to play any solos, but had a great time tooting away with my buddies. Our music was pretty awful by the standards of today's high school bands.

With our family tradition of singing at home, vocal music was especially appealing to me. Over the four high school years I sang in the mixed chorus, boy's glee club, mixed quartet, male quartet and a special eight-voice group. As a freshman my voice hadn't changed and I sang soprano along with the girls when I didn't think the director would notice.

I somehow had the idea that good singing was loud singing. After our first mixed chorus concert I learned an embarrassing lesson. Our principal, Mr. George Riley, had attended the concert. The next day in his freshman civics class he was addressing the subject of cooperation. He said, "Last night at the program there was one tenor who sang much louder than anybody else. He needs to learn to blend with the group." He glanced in my direction but mercifully didn't identify me. I was mortified and certain that everybody recognized that he was talking about me. Thereafter I turned down my volume and tried to blend with those around me.

We all looked forward to attending and participating in the spring music contests with other high schools. A big part of the fun and excitement came from the bus ride with all of our friends. We particularly enjoyed meeting the students from other schools and hearing them perform. Groups who performed well at the regional contests were invited to go to the state music festival.

In 1941 our mixed chorus participated in the state contest in Columbia. My brother Paul was a freshman there at the University of Missouri. He was living in a rental room in the back of a shoemaker's shop. We had a two-hour break at noon before our performance and two friends went with me to visit Paul. On the way we had to jump over a large puddle.

In stretching out during my leap I ripped the back of my good pants wide open exposing a broad expanse of white underwear. I gingerly walked on to Paul's room and explained my dilemma. He looked for a needle and thread. The shoemaker became aware of my problem and said, "Hey! I can fix that! Take off your trousers and give them to me." I complied and he sewed them up on his heavy-duty shoemaker's sewing machine. That was one seam which never ripped apart again. We got back to the auditorium just in time to sing with our chorus.

My secret ambition was to sing solos but my self-consciousness totally thwarted my performing alone in the presence of other people. For the first three years of high school I refused to try out for any solo parts. In my senior year, when I heard others singing alone, I started thinking, "Why, I could do better than that!" One day I overheard Mr. Mcdonald, the current music teacher, say, "John Hult has a good voice but he's too inhibited to ever sing a solo." I decided to show him otherwise. My opportunity came at the end of the year. A committee asked for a volunteer from our graduating class to sing at our alumni banquet and I held up my hand. I was still terribly apprehensive. I selected the then-popular, "Let's Remember Pearl Harbor!"

I practiced and practiced: while I was milking the cows, feeding the chickens, or walking a mile to the bus-stop. On the appointed night my big moment finally arrived. My knees were wobbly as I stood up. The accompanist played the introduction and I belted out those immortal lyrics:

Let's remember Pearl Harbor as we go to meet the foe.
Let's remember Pearl Harbor as we did the Alamo.
We will always remember how they died for liberty.
Let's remember Pearl Harbor and go on to victory!

That broke the ice. There was an encouraging round of applause. I've jumped at every opportunity to sing since that debut. I took voice lessons in college and sang solos with an army glee club in Texas. In my first two years of medical school I got a job as tenor soloist in a church in St. Louis for ten dollars a week. That was enough to pay for my food in those days. Years later my greatest musical thrill was auditioning for and winning the privilege of singing the tenor solos of Handel's Messiah with a large community chorus in Colorado.

Today I'm a bit frustrated that my voice is definitely over the hill. That doesn't keep me from enjoying singing with our church choir and The O.K. Chorale, a group of senior citizens whose average age is nearly eighty. O.K. stands for 'Older Kids.'

Vocal music is still an important facet of my life. I will always remember that it began with our mother leading our family in singing around our old reed organ before bedtime. The thrill of singing was then enriched and amplified during my four years at Rogersville High School.

A HAPPY SUMMER IN MICHIGAN

In 1940 Daddy was serving as temporary pastor to two Lutheran congregations in Rapid River and Stonington on the beautiful Upper Peninsula of Michigan. He was lonesome for his family. His parishioners in Stonington suggested that he bring his wife and 10 children up for the summer. One member of the congregation had a large empty house which we could occupy. Daddy wrote to mother discussing this possibility. But how could we leave Bethany Homestead? Who would care for the animals and the orchard? A member of our home church in Springfield suggested that his two teen-aged sons didn't have summer jobs and were looking for something to keep them occupied. We knew the Schultz boys well, and considered them to be completely trustworthy. Mother made an agreement with them that their income would be all the money realized from our cream, eggs and whatever apples and vinegar they could sell. We informed our neighbors of this arrangement and put in a summer's supply of feed for the livestock. The Schultz boys would come and occupy our home the day we departed for Michigan. Their parents would visit them regularly for supervision and moral support.

After Paul's high school graduation and the beginning of summer vacation, there were feverish days of preparation for our big trip. Mother and the older sisters spent much time sewing and mending. Believe it or not, Paul and I had been taught to darn our own socks so the women of the family didn't have to worry about that little chore. Many other details were dealt with, including meticulously servicing our car.

When the big day of our departure came up on the calendar our excitement had reached fever pitch. Paul was our only licensed driver and keenly felt the responsibility of chauffeuring us nearly 1000 miles north. He made last minute checks of the tires and under the hood. He and Mother carefully strapped much of our luggage on the large running boards on both sides of the car. With these loads the only door which could be opened was that of the driver. We then began the process of cramming 11 Hults into the old 1927 Packard which Mother's Uncle Charley had given us two years earlier. Ingrid and I sat in the back seat with Mary, four, and Gustav, six, between us. Carl, Martha and Eunice perched on small folding jump seats between the front and back seats. Mother had to squeeze under the steering wheel to get to her seat in the right front. Veda, twelve, crawled in beside her next to the driver. Finally Paul gently lifted 2-year-old David through the window onto Mother's lap and then settled into the driver's seat. We were ready to embark! Thank God we didn't have to worry about seat belts. But wait a minute! I was to be the navigator and had forgotten the maps. We would never be able to find our way without them. I crawled out the left back window and ran into the house to retrieve them. I rushed back to the car and eased my 160-pound frame through the window again. And away we went! (I must acknowledge that I obtained some of the details of this eventful departure from Ingrid's family biography On Our Way Rejoicing published by Harper and Row in 1964.)

We were all proud of Paul's careful and skillful driving. We didn't have a car radio, but not to worry. We could create our own music. We sang every song and hymn we knew over and over again. Pit stops were frequent and complicated with only one openable door. Every time we rode through town we were greeted with unbelieving stares as Mother, plus six blonde and four red heads could be counted through the windows. Ingrid, at a dignified 14 years, was embarrassed at the spectacle we created. For my part, I wasn't bothered at all and enjoyed waving at the gawkers.

After we got north of the Missouri River we began passing through the wonderfully rich farmlands of the 'American Breadbasket' of Northern Missouri and Illinois. Miles and miles of lush green fields of corn, soybeans and other crops contrasted with what we were accustomed to on the poor soil of the Ozarks. When we started touring through the gently rolling dairyland of Wisconsin studded with many lakes and evergreen forests I almost felt like we were entering paradise. We overnighted in rustic tourist cabins, the predecessors of motels. After we passed Green Bay we looked out on magnificent vistas of Lake Michigan, the first time in my memory in which we could see water clear to the distant horizon.

After three days on the road we reached our summer home in Stonington and were thrilled to have Daddy rush out to greet us. Mother got the first hug, then each of us had our turn in Daddy's arms. Tears of joy were shed and happy laughter highlighted our first moments of reunion. We entered the large house and found that the ladies of the church had made up beds for all of us and prepared a delicious hot meal. After hot baths we were all ready for bed. This was the first time all 12 of us had slept under the same roof, since the limited space of our tiny house in Missouri had dictated separate sleeping quarters for the older children, a converted smokehouse and a refurbished chicken-house. That first night in Stonington as we drifted off to sleep the last thing I remember hearing was the happy conversation of our parents.

In the morning we brothers excitedly explored our neighborhood. Our house stood on a bluff overlooking Little Bay de Noc, on Lake Michigan. The waves lapped against a narrow beach just a hundred yards from our summer home. Our nearest neighbor was Mr. Hanson, a fisherman who kept his boat at a dock just south of us. Paul and I were thrilled when he invited us to go out with him to check his nets that morning. We helped him harvest three large fish boxes of whitefish. He was disappointed that there was only one lake trout and explained that lamprey eels had decimated the population of that species. He also invited us to use one of his rowboats to fish for yellow perch just offshore near an old stone jetty. We had several opportunities to do that during the summer.

Seven miles across the bay we could see the city of Escanaba with its huge iron ore docks. To us landlubbers it was exciting to watch the ore carriers sailing in with their hulks high out of the water and later departing heavily laden. The blasts from their horns made a wonderful full-throated sound which could be heard for miles.

Two of the Stonington farmers invited Paul and me to help them with their hay harvest. My lot fell to spend many days working for Joe Peterson, a jolly little man who became a special friend. He and his wife Ebba had no children and they sort of adopted me. Most of the haying was accomplished using a powerful team of draft horses. Joe didn't have a hay baler so one of us pitched the loose hay up to the other on the wagon. I was taller than he so I usually ended up on the ground. He said that I could keep up with any of his previous hired hands. His loft space in the barn was limited so it was important to spread the hay into every corner. I gravitated into that responsibility and Joe said that I packed in more hay than he had ever stored for the winter. His appreciation was good for my morale.

One day in the loft I slipped and fell forward impaling my right thigh with the pitchfork. One tine of the fork entered the front of my right thigh and came out the side three inches back. The pain was awful. I gritted my teeth, pulled the fork out and went right on working without telling Joe of my mishap. He would have been very upset and worried about me. Furthermore we were behind schedule for the day and rain clouds were approaching. And I certainly didn't tell Mother knowing her anxiety about tetanus, or lockjaw as we usually called it. My leg was sore for a few days but didn't get infected. Apparently my guardian angel was watching over me.

When Joe Peterson discovered that I had a background of milking cows for almost a decade he recruited me to assist him in his dairy operation. He did not have a mechanical milking machine to accommodate his small herd of ten gentle Jerseys. Timing required that his milk be ready for pick-up before we went out to bring in the hay. I was able to walk from our summer home across the alfalfa field to his farm at 6:00 AM. Several times I surprised deer feeding on the alfalfa. I was thrilled to watch them daintily hop away and disappear into the woods when they sensed my presence. When I reached the Peterson home Ebba always had the coffeepot on and we all three had a leisurely cup before Joe and I went to the barn. Joe was surprised that I could fill my pail with milk faster than he.

Ebba had a special cat who always put in an appearance when we began milking. She meowed until one of us would squirt milk into her mouth. I noticed that she was highly pregnant. She slept in the barn loft. One morning while milking I heard her yowling above me. As she jumped down either to get her breakfast or to find a better place to have her babies, I was astounded to see a kitten pop out of the mother's body right in front of me in mid-air. That's the only occasion on which I have witnessed a mammalian creature born while its mother was flying unsupported through the air. (I wonder if we will ever have a lady astronaut bearing a child while weightless in space.) The feline mother picked up the newborn kitty in her mouth and carried it away.

About half the Stonington community was populated with Norwegians and the other half, Swedes; and there wasn't much love lost between the two groups. There was a Norwegian Lutheran church just down the road from our Swedish Lutheran church and we never had joint worship services. They had each worshipped in their native languages when their churches were first established. In 1940 they still maintained some of this linguistic diversity. Our morning services were in English but Daddy regularly preached Swedish sermons for the older people on certain Sundays. Joe Peterson said that he actually spoke more eloquently in Swedish. I enjoyed listening to his down-to-earth English language sermons. He was never a fiery, arm-waving preacher. He used anecdotes and stories from everyday life to illustrate his messages. He preached much like he would have visited with a friend across the table over a cup of coffee. I remember his delivery as being somewhat hesitant as if he was searching for just the right word. He projected an image of strength but also kindness, gentleness, and humility. I was proud and grateful that he was my father.

Our 1927 Packard with heavily laden running board. David, 2, in the passenger seat. Paul, 18, by the driver's door.

All twelve of us lived under one roof for the first time.

Farewell Celebration, with Paul absent!

A Norwegian family, the Pedersens, had the only store in Stonington with a limited supply of groceries and daily essentials. They also had a teenage daughter Margaret who was about the most beautiful creature I had ever seen. I remember looking for excuses to go shopping just so I could gaze at her in awe. Six years later I was back in Stonington after my first year in medical school. Margaret was even more beautiful but had a fine Norwegian husband and a handsome little blonde toddler son.

Whenever there was time I would dig a can of earthworms, borrow Mr. Hanson's rowboat, row out to the end of the old jetty, anchor and catch a mess of yellow perch. Nine-year-old brother Carl really enjoyed going along with me. One day we went down to the dock and found the waves too high to venture out. A Polish immigrant Stonington resident who often fished near us was also there bemoaning the unsatisfactory fishing conditions. In his limited and heavily accented English he declared, "Too much water jump!!" Carl and I had a hard time to keep from laughing. After another of our fishing expeditions, I failed to tie up the boat securely and it drifted away. A south wind blew it 15 miles northward to Rapid River where it washed up on a beach. The sheriff was understandably concerned about possible drownings. There was enough information on the boat to indicate its owner and the authorities were relieved to ascertain that nobody had gone overboard. I was terribly embarrassed but after the boat had been retrieved Mr. Hanson insisted that I should keep on using it. Believe me, I made sure to tie up carefully thereafter.

Daddy's other church was located in Rapid River, 15 miles north of Stonington, at the head of Little Bay de Noc. The parishioners were a little more sophisticated and proud of their lovely brick church. Our Stonington church was smaller and built of local pine lumber. When we worshipped in Rapid River, Paul, Ingrid, Veda and I sang with the choir and mingled with the other teenagers. A pretty girl named Edith and Paul were mutually attracted to each other and spent as much time together as possible. Toward the end of the summer the Rapid River congregation had a special potluck dinner and farewell celebration for our family after church on Sunday morning. Daddy wanted us all to be on hand, but Paul, Edith and several other young friends had made plans for a separate celebration of their own. Our dear father was upset that he couldn't have all 10 of his children on hand but the young people prevailed and went on their way. I believe that Mother argued on their behalf but Daddy was still a bit disgruntled and muttered something about 'puppy love.' At 18 he hadn't even had the privilege of starting high school and Paul was already going off to the University of Missouri. Our Papa was especially disappointed when our family was assembled for a picture. I too loved my family but would have been happier to be off with the older teenagers. I can now understand Daddy's deep disappointment. That was our very last full family photo opportunity and one handsome son was missing.

The end of our idyllic summer was drawing to a close. The Schultz boys had done well at Bethany Homestead but were anxious to be relieved. A date was set for our departure. In Stonington Joe Peterson wondered if it would be possible for me to stay for a few extra days to help him finish haying. I pleaded with my parents for permission and suggested that I could hitchhike back to Missouri. I argued that there would be more room in the old Packard and that Daddy would have at least one member of the family with him for a few more days. At first Mother was reluctant but finally agreed. I believe my proposed hitchhiking expedition appealed to Daddy's adventurous spirit. He would have jumped at the chance when he was 16 years old. So the decision was made and Mother and nine of her brood of ten departed southward. Three days later she called from Springfield to report their safe arrival.

I really cherished the next two weeks alone with my Dad. That was the only time ever in which I didn't have to share his love and attention with a multitude of siblings. We had some great visits and I was especially moved when we had our morning devotions and prayers together. We always began by singing one of our family favorite hymns, "Again Thy Glorious Sun Doth Rise." He always concluded with a prayer which included each one of his family by name. He was a pretty good cook too but his parishioners saw that we enjoyed several home-cooked suppers in their homes.

I made one contribution to our diet during those last two weeks. I knew that Daddy liked fish in any form, especially the smoked variety. Joe Peterson volunteered to help me with my project. I dug a canful of earthworms, went out in the boat and caught about 30 fat yellow perch. Joe and I cleaned them and soaked them overnight in brine. The following day we put them in his unique smoking system. It consisted of an upright 50-gallon steel drum with a 4-inch drainpipe into the bottom. The pipe was covered with a few inches of soil and led to a firepit six feet away. We started a fire of birch wood which sent up a nice cloud of smoke. A ventilation shaft led the smoke into the barrel. The fish were suspended from a lattice of wire across the top of the barrel which was covered with burlap. We kept a slow fire going and after two days had a nice batch of golden brown smoked perch. We enjoyed them over the next few days and I was delighted with Daddy's hungry enthusiasm.

All good things must come to an end. The day arrived when I needed to head for home. Joe paid me my wages of $1.50 per day which was more than I had ever received in Missouri for even longer workdays. Ebba fed me a delicious breakfast and we shared an emotional farewell. I promised them that I would return and help them again another summer. That resolution was fulfilled six years later after I got out of the army and completed my exhausting freshman year in medical school.

I packed my belongings in a small suitcase and Daddy drove me 30 miles around Little Bay de Noc to Escanaba. He let me off at the highway to Green Bay, gave me a big hug and we both shed a few tears. There was some trepidation as I looked southward and wondered if I really appreciated the situation into which I was putting myself. Daddy waited within sight until he saw a driver stop and pick me up. He must have had at least a little anxiety as he watched his 16-year-old son heading off alone.

I enjoyed visiting with each of the friendly drivers who picked me up. By nightfall of that first day I reached Rockford, Illinois. My last ride took me into the downtown Swedish section of the city. After checking into a modest hotel I went out to a nearby restaurant and splurged on a 50-cent meal which featured Swedish meatballs. Much of the conversation of my fellow diners was in Swedish and I regretted that our parents hadn't seen fit to teach us our ethnic tongue. Back in my room I soon read myself to sleep.

The following morning I rode a streetcar to the edge of town. My first day's good hitchhiking didn't carry over and by late afternoon I had traversed less than 200 miles. I waited for a ride for over an hour on the edge of Beardstown, Illinois. Two large weird-looking middle-aged men came out of their house, and waddled out to visit with me. In retrospect I'm sure they had Down's syndrome. Never before had I been close to anybody like those two. I was really scared of them and couldn't understand what they were trying to tell me. Soon their elderly mother appeared and recognized my uneasiness. She reassured me that they were trying to be friendly and asked me where I was going. When she heard that I was over 300 miles from my Missouri home she insisted that I sleep overnight in her guest bedroom. I was still uneasy about her sons but accepted her kind offer. My Mother would have issued the same invitation. My kind hostess fed me a hearty supper and I slept well in a clean bed. After a good breakfast in the morning I insisted on paying her but she wouldn't hear of it. I thanked her profusely, shook hands with her sons and walked out to the highway. My guardian angel had looked out for me in the person of this kind and generous lady. Would something like that still happen in today's world?

My final day on the road went smoothly. I had planned my route to cross the Mississippi at Hannibal, Missouri in order to bypass St. Louis and to get a peek at Mark Twain's hometown. My first ride that morning took me well into Missouri. Back in my home state after two months away! I was intrigued to observe the difference of accents of the drivers who had picked me up along the way. The farther north people spoke faster with clipped consonants and often a Scandinavian or German flavor. That gradually changed as I got farther south. A couple more rides got me into the Ozarks, back to that slow drawl and unique vocabulary. Before sundown I was in Springfield. I called Mother to announce my safe arrival and

Paul drove in to pick me up in the old Packard. We had enjoyed a marvelous summer but it was great to be back in the hills of home with family and friends.

HIGH SCHOOL GRADUATION

In April of 1942 our high school principal called me into his office. "What have I done now?" I thought. He greeted me with a big smile and said, "Congratulations! It has been officially determined that you are the valedictorian of this year's graduating class!" I knew that I was in the running but thought that one of my classmates had passed me up during the previous semester. Naturally I was pleased and excited, and yes, just a little bit proud. Then came the bad news. Mr. Hamilton informed me that I would be expected to prepare and deliver a valedictory address of about 10 minutes duration. The subject would be up to me and I was not to solicit help from anybody on the faculty. Public speaking was not my forte and I was petrified.

I didn't sleep well that night. What was I going to proclaim to the world on graduation day? Of course, because of the war my speech had to have an element of patriotic fervor. The Pearl Harbor disaster had occurred just five months earlier and our nation was totally involved in a global war. Some of my classmates had already volunteered and were in uniform. I knew that I would soon be drafted. I decided to entitle my address, "Our Faith is in America!"

Over the next two weeks I wrote and rewrote what I was going to say. At first nothing seemed right and I was terribly unsure of myself. Finally things started coming together. I wrote out my final draft and committed it to memory. I practiced my delivery while milking the cows morning and evening. They listened politely and my rendition didn't curdle the milk. Since I had to walk a mile to catch the bus, I also utilized that opportunity to declare my message to the hills of the Ozarks. My confidence was building.

I was delighted that my father was going to be able to attend my graduation. He was supposed to have been in Africa. As a missionary pastor he had sailed early in 1941 to help in an emergency situation in Tanganyika. The German missionaries had been deported by the British, leaving their churches leaderless. My Dad had been asked to help fill this vacuum. He was one of 125 American missionaries traveling on the Egyptian ship the ZamZam to several African destinations. The ship was shelled and sunk by a German raider vessel. All passengers were rescued and carried through the British blockade to Occupied France. Since the United States was not yet at war the Americans were released through Portugal and returned home. After several weeks of rest and recuperation at home Daddy began making arrangements to return to Africa. He was scheduled to leave soon after my graduation.

About two weeks before the big day, he asked me if he could see my speech and possibly make suggestions. I wasn't sure that I wanted him to tamper with my masterpiece but out of love and respect handed him my manuscript. He wrote in a few simple suggestions which I can now see made the message clearer and easier to deliver. I incorporated them and memorized the revised text.

At last the great night arrived, May 15, 1942. The high school gym was packed. My spine tingled as I looked out at my smiling parents. I was grateful to them for all the times they had helped me with my homework or said, "John, this is a good report card but you can do even better." Surrounding my parents were five of my younger brothers and sisters. When it was my time to speak my 4-year-old brother David looked up at me and grinned. That was just what I needed to help me relax. I stood up, walked briskly to the speaker's podium, cleared my throat and began:

Ladies and Gentlemen,

As we the seniors of Rogersville High School come before you tonight as candidates for graduation we find ourselves face to face with many confusing problems and doubts. In this troubled world what are we to believe? In what can we place our trust? High school graduates of today look anxiously into the future. What does it have in store for us? The whole world seems to be in the throes of a violent earthquake. The entire globe seems to have been rent in twain. Mankind today finds itself divided into two huge factions fighting a titanic duel to the bitter end. One is seeking to destroy and the other to preserve the ideals which we cherish. Although there is little stability in the world today, there is one thing in which we can firmly believe and that is our great country. America will stand firm and come through these testings and trials.

Many years ago our Pilgrim forefathers faced much more imposing obstacles in their great enterprise of founding this nation. Led by their faith in a noble cause they succeeded and their efforts and sacrifices were continued by a host of patriots in all the intervening years. Many of our own ancestors came across the ocean and played their roles in a variety of ways. America, through their strong faith and united efforts, has become the greatest nation on earth. It is now up to us to preserve it as such.

When we look back over the remarkable development of America we remember her great discoverer Christopher Columbus. His faith in a particular dream brought forth fruit a million-fold. When he was still a boy he dreamed happy visions of wonderful lands across the sea and he was determined even then to find them. Striving forward through seemingly insurmountable odds he finally realized his lofty ambitions. His dreams came true far exceeding his youthful visions in their ultimate value.

Columbus' discovery would have been insignificant had it not been for those brave men and women who followed him. On a cold December day in 1620 that first little band of Pilgrims set foot on the shores of New England. Why had they left their homes in England to come to these inhospitable shores? Had they come for adventure's sake? Were they seeking fabulous fortunes in gold? No! They came so that they and their descendants might worship God according to the dictates of their conscience. They came in order to be released from the bonds of restricted speech and publication. They came so that they might be free and no longer virtual slaves in a feudal society.

From 1620 until today America has grown and prospered. Millions of people oppressed by the inequalities of the Old World saw in America a haven of refuge. They were welcomed to experience the blessings of liberty and equality. Their united efforts transformed this vast undeveloped domain into the greatest nation on the globe. The noble ideals which brought our ancestors here were preserved and extended. Led by the faith and courage of George Washington, Benjamin Franklin, Thomas Jefferson, Abraham Lincoln and many others our land has become the envy of all nations.

Today as we look back on the development of our country we cannot help but be concerned about her future. The United States has become the bulwark of democracy in the world. Can we preserve that state in this time of crisis? Our answer is a unanimous "Yes!" The future of America will soon rest on our shoulders and we are determined to carry the torch. Our land today is a land at war. We are just one of an alliance of 23 liberty-seeking nations.

We are all determined to crush the tyranny of dictatorship and once again bring freedom and equality to the world. What part are we as individuals to play in this struggle? Each of us has a role to play. We may serve in the armed forces, we may produce food, we may work in factories or serve as homemakers, teachers, secretaries, etc. All are equally important and interdependent. Let us remember that for every man on the front line in battle there must be many men and women to back him up, to feed him, to clothe him, to nurse him, and to supply him with the materials with which to fight. Although most of us will never bear arms we are all essential members of the team. Let us then put our shoulders to the wheel, let us give, let us fight if that is our lot. Let us put our whole souls and bodies into the struggle, that America through our faith and effort might live on as a great free land.

And now in conclusion I bid each of my classmates and fellow students a fond farewell which in a sense is not a farewell. Though we have come to a place in the trail where our ways must separate, we will all be moving in the same direction, namely service to our country. Though we each will be performing different tasks each will be spinning a necessary separate strand. These will all be united into a great cable which will pull America through her trials to victory.

To our teachers we say "Thank you!" For the past four years you have been leading us along the paths of acquiring knowledge and understanding. You have taught us many of the skills which we need on the road ahead. To you we express sincere gratitude for the fundamental roles you have played in our lives.

To our parents we do not say farewell but pay you a tribute which words alone cannot express. You began leading us along the right paths before we could walk, talk or remember. On through the years you have guided our wayward steps with your firm but loving hands. You have sacrificed more than we will ever know. We can only say, "Thank you from the bottom of our hearts!"

As I sat down I took a deep breath and said to myself, "Wow I made it!" Now over 50 years later as I reread my yellowed handwritten manuscript vivid memories come surging back. I cherish the vision of my Dad's presence that night and his final editing of my address. A few weeks later he sailed for Africa and, in less than a year, died of malaria and heart failure in Dar es Salaam. I am grateful to my wonderful Mother for saving my speech manuscript and many other mementos and for always being there when I most needed her.

Today as I critically review what I wrote over a half-century ago, I wonder how I ever passed English grammar. I'm a little amused at my youthful naiveté and fervor, and surprised at some of my profound pontifications. Obviously our history books didn't give much credit to Native Americans, Black slaves from Africa, or the Spanish and French founders of our country.

That graduation night, May 15, 1942, furnished one of the most exciting and exhilarating experiences of my life.

PEARL HARBOR—WORLD WAR II— FAREWELL TO THE OZARKS

On Sunday afternoon Dec. 7, 1941, I was out walking in the woods near Bethany Homestead. We were enjoying a beautiful Ozark fall day with shirtsleeve temperature. When I realized that it was time to start the evening chores I headed homeward. Nearing the house I heard excited voices. One of my sisters hurried out to tell me that the Japanese were dropping bombs on American ships in Hawaii. We were shocked to hear that much of the American fleet had been destroyed with much loss of life. We listened intently to President Roosevelt's dramatic 'Day of Infamy' speech, and our country was soon engulfed in World War II. Our world would never be the same again.

All of us were caught up in a contagious patriotic fervor and righteous anger against Japan and Germany. On Pearl Harbor day I was seventeen and a half years old, six months shy of draft age and eagerly anticipating military service. Some of my classmates dropped everything and enlisted but I was convinced that it was extremely important to finish my senior year in high school. Our big brother Paul had not returned to the University of Missouri for his sophomore year. He went to work in a defense industry-based job in Rock Island, Illinois. Before his draft number came up he enlisted in the Marine Corps.

Soon after my graduation from high school Daddy returned to Tanganyika. He sailed on a merchant ship laden with munitions. Mother and my younger siblings probably would have gone with him if the war hadn't made sea travel so dangerous. Daddy landed in South Africa and journeyed by rail and bus north to Tanganyika. He was thrilled to be back after a 14-year absence.

These events left me as the man of the house with Mother and my eight younger brothers and sisters. As the valedictorian of my high school class I was awarded a full-tuition scholarship to Southwest Missouri State Teachers College in Springfield. At that time full-tuition added up to only $100 per year. At Mother's insistence I enrolled in spite of the impending draft. I had registered after my birthday in June and was told that I wouldn't be called up until late winter. When school began I got up at 5:00 AM, did my chores, and rode my bicycle five miles to the campus. I took a full academic load of English composition, chemistry, Latin, and math. I enjoyed my courses and completed the fall trimester.

Since I was in college I went to the Navy recruiting office to investigate the possibility of getting into the college V-12 program. On a preliminary physical examination the doctor checked out my badly decayed front teeth and indicated that my dental health was unacceptable for naval officer's training.

Before my draft notice came Mother and I talked about seeking a deferment as a farm worker. Our little orchard farm wasn't productive enough to really qualify, but Mother could have made a strong case to keep me at home with her large brood of small children. She insisted that I should be free to make my own choice because she knew how badly I wanted to be in the service. She said that with three teen-age sisters and 12-year-old brother Carl they could make out. I have always been grateful for that totally unselfish decision on her part.

I started the winter trimester at STC but experienced great difficulty in concentrating on my studies. What was the use of that effort when going to the army was inevitable. In mid-January I received my 'greetings' letter from President Roosevelt which invited me to present myself at Ft. Leavenworth, Kansas, on Feb. 1st for my induction physical examination. I was genuinely eager to be in the service, to be away from home, and to forge an identity for myself. I fantasized that I would become a great hero in the mold of Gary Cooper as Sergeant York of World War I. On the other hand, this would be the first time I had been away from the warmth, love and security of home and family. I also felt a measure of guilt that I was deserting Mother and my brothers and sisters when Daddy was already in Africa and Paul on the way to the South Pacific in the Marine Corps.

Those last two weeks of civilian life were consumed by feverish preparations. I was able to take examinations and get credit for two of my courses, physics and Latin. My voice teacher, Agnes Dade Cowan, shed a few tears after conducting my last voice lesson. She felt that I had definite possibilities as a singer. One day I rode the bus to Rogersville to bid farewell to high school teachers and friends. Carl and I sawed enough firewood with our big old crosscut saw to keep the family warm the rest of the winter. On another day I went to the tire store. The rationing board had given us a certificate authorizing the purchase of five badly needed new tires for our car. I went with Mother to get her first ever driver's license. All she had to do was answer a few questions and pay fifty cents. There was no driving performance examination. Actually she soon became probably the best driver in the family. Our mother could do just about anything to which she set her mind.

The big day arrived. According to my diary I climbed on a bus just after midnight on Feb. 1st and we headed for Ft. Leavenworth. I was too excited to sleep. After changing busses in Kansas City we arrived at the induction center at 9:30 AM. We new recruits were immediately herded into a large dispensary where we were turned over to the doctors and non-commissioned medics. We were ordered to take off all of our clothes and stand in line. I remembered my Dad telling of similar indignities he had endured during an army physical exam in 1917. (He passed the examination but was deferred as a seminary student). We were listened to with cold stethoscopes, poked, prodded and all body openings were inspected. My examining doctor called over a colleague to check a minor deviation from normal on my body. They could see that I was anxious so one of them immediately said, "Don't get excited! This won't keep you out! As long as you are warm and breathing Uncle Sam will take you!" So I passed that obstacle course and spent the rest of the afternoon filling out forms and standing in various lines.

At 6:00 PM our group was assembled in an auditorium and sworn in as privates in the United States Army. I was impressed by the dignity and gravity of the ceremony, but wondered when and if I would ever get to see my family again. Then the officer in charge said "You are all on furlough for a week. Go home. Wind up your affairs and be back on the 8th. We'll be waiting for you." I was a little disappointed that we weren't issued uniforms for that last week of freedom. After that momentous day we were hungry. I headed to the mess hall for a hearty meal, then got in line for the bus back to Springfield and a final round of farewells.

My last week at home slipped by rapidly. There were a few tear-jerking farewells, but I was eager to be on my way. I didn't have any serious girlfriends but there were a couple to whom I hated to say goodbye for the duration. I visited high school again and attended a couple of my college classes. On the last day a tour of our neighborhood enabled me to make final visits to special friends. On the last night at home I lay awake for two hours excitedly anticipating the dramatic change in my life.

On February 8, 1943, I arose at 5:30 and had breakfast with Mother, Carl and David. They brought me to the bus depot in Springfield and waited with me until my bus departed at 8:00. Through the window I could see that Mother was crying and I'm certain that my cheeks were moist also. In my diary I wrote, "It was kinda' tough saying goodbye to Mother and my brothers but I'm eager to get into it." My dear brave mother had already waved goodbye to the love of her life when he departed for Africa. She would never see him again. Then she bade farewell to her oldest son Paul as he went off to the US Marines. Now she was releasing me to go off to an unknown fate in the army. And the little boy inside me was crying out, "How am I going to get along without her presence, her comforting love?"

So-o-o—my days of growing up in the Ozarks were coming to an end. A whole new world awaited me. My parents had instilled in us the belief that God had a plan for each of us and I was determined to keep in touch with Him. For the immediate future I was going to be the best soldier I could be.

Carl and I sawing firewood.   Private John Hult, US Army.

Our last family photo with Daddy, 1940. Front row: Gus, Daddy, Mary, David, Mother, Paul. Back row: Martha, Carl, Ingrid, John, Veda, Eunice. The signature is Daddy's handwriting.

Quiet Waters Publications

Bolivar MO 65613-0034 www.quietwaterspub.com:

Daktari Yohana

By John Hult

John Hult was born to missionary parents on the slope of Kilimanjaro in 1924. He left Africa at age two, returning thirty-three years later to work as a physician. In his humorous and intimate style John Hult tells captivating stories about his four years in Tanzania as a missionary doctor.
ISBN 0-9663966-5-0

Miracle at Sea

Eleanor Anderson

In 1941, before America was at war with Germany, a German raider sunk the Egyptian liner Zamzam in the South Atlantic. On board of the vessel were more than 120 American missionaries, among them Mrs. Lillian Danielson and her six children. Eleanor, who was then only nine years old, presents a detailed account of the family's departure from America, the catastrophe, and the distressing and arduous voyage back to safety.
ISBN 1-931475-05-9

On Our Way Rejoicing

By Ingrid Trobisch

Ralph Hult had embarked on the ill-fated *Zamzam* as well. After returning to the US he set out for Tanzania the following year where he died unexpectedly. His daughter, Ingrid Trobisch, tells the story of what happens when God takes away the father of ten children. A whole family is called to service and sent into the world. The story surges with movement, partings and reunion, sorrows and joys, adventure and romance, shining courage, and above all, the warm love that knits together a large Christian family.
ISBN 0-9663966-2-6

Touched by the African Soul

Compiled by Gloria Cunningham & Lois Okerstrom
A collection of short stories, written by sixty-two missionary women who recall their adventuresome years in Tanzania. The stories tell of personal experiences of the writers and give insight into the culture and Christian faith of the Tanzanian people among whom they lived and worked.
ISBN 0-9663966-9-3

Passport to Borneo

By Adeline Hult
In 1951 Adeline Hult was called as a missionary teacher to work with a Chinese church in British North Borneo. This is her story of the four years she worked there during the years of restoration after World War II. She shares her experiences of living abroad for the first time and the joys, frustrations, and adaptations necessary to cope with life in a multi-cultural colony. Upon her return she married Dr. John Hult.

The Adventures Of Pumpelhoober

By David Trobisch, illustrated by Eva Bruchmann
"In Austria they call someone who has a lot of bad luck, 'Pumpelhoober'. I, too, often have bad luck," nine year old David explains his nickname. This humorous children's book tells the story of the Trobisch family in Africa from the perspective of a child.
ISBN 0-9663966-4-2

I Married You

By Walter Trobisch
Set in a large African city, this story covers only four days in the life of Walter and Ingrid Trobisch. Nothing in this book is fiction. All the events have really happened. The people involved are still living today. The direct, sensitive, and compassionate narrative presents Christian marriage as a dynamic triangle.
ISBN 0-9663966-6-9

I Loved A Girl

By Walter Trobisch

'Last Friday, I loved a girl – or as you would put it, I committed adultery.' This deeply moving story of a young African couple has become a worldwide classic with its frank answers to frank questions about sex and love. Its tremendous success led Walter and Ingrid Trobisch to leave their missionary post in Cameroun and start an international ministry as marriage and family counselors.

ISBN 0-9663966-0-X

Singing I Go

By Beryl Ramsey Sand

She heard the Spirit's call to serve as a missionary at the age of fifteen. Ten years later, in May of 1944 and in the midst of World War II, Beryl arrived in Africa. She worked as a nurse, as a literacy teacher, and she assisted in writing the first Bible teaching material in the Gbaya language. In this book Beryl chronicles her life through her memories and letters.

ISBN 1-931475-02-4

www.ingramcontent.com/pod-product-compliance
Lightning Source LLC
Chambersburg PA
CBHW031256110426
42743CB00039B/417